Preaching
the
Four Faces
of
Salvation

by Steven P. Vitrano, Ph.D.

To my wife, Charlene,
who has been the love of my
life and companion in
ministry for more than 50
years, this book is dedicated.
She was the first reader and
editor of the manuscript, and
to her I am most grateful.

Contents

Introduction

This book is about preaching the doctrine of salvation in its fullness. Like a precious jewel the doctrine has several facets or "faces." These facets—reconciliation, transformation, glorification, and restoration—make known to us the best, the greatest, the most thrilling and wonderful "good news" in all of its glory.

While the book is about preaching, it is not a homiletics text. The chapters are not intended to be model sermons, but rather written proclamations of the gospel by one who has preached and taught preaching throughout his professional career.

Of all the Christians who believe in righteousness by faith, not all agree as to what that means. This is most unfortunate because, of the truths revealed in Scripture, this is by far the most important. It strikes me as quite tragic that while we may have discovered the "truth" on all the other Bible doctrines, including the interpretation of all the symbolic prophecies, we remain confused when it comes to the doctrine of salvation.

Perhaps it is because of my training in communication that I suspect at least part of our problem comes from a lack of clarity in the language we use and how we use it. What about the context in which we use the word "saved"? Are we as clear and coherent as we could be? Do we hear and understand the same thing even when we all use the same word?

Or is our confusion also due to the fact that in much of our preaching, discussion, and dialogue we don't deal with the doctrine of salvation holistically? We focus on this aspect or that aspect and fail to consider that a part is often truly understood only in the light of the whole. Which is why one of the first principles in biblical interpretation is, "Let the Bible interpret itself." Which is to say, let the meaning of a passage be found in the larger context—chapter, book, or all of Scripture.

That is why this book is a Bible study. It is written under the conviction that, when properly used, God's Word interprets itself. Thus, many texts of Scripture are used, some more than once, and some quoted at length. That is also why other sources are not used except those which help clarify words and language usage, especially in the New Testament.

The sources: *The Greek New Testament,* fourth revised edition, published by the United Bible Societies, 1994; *The Analytical Greek Lexicon,* published by Harper and Brothers and Samuel Bagster and Sons, London; *The New Analytical Greek Lexicon,* edited by Wesley J. Perschbacher, published by Hendrickson of Peabody, Massachusetts, 1994; and *Young's Analytical Concordance to the Bible,* published by Wm. B. Eerdmans, Grand Rapids, Michigan.

I know very well that a flood of articles, books, and sermons on the subject of righteousness by faith have been published and preached in the last century. Some would say, "Enough is enough." Yet as long as the polarization between "cheap grace" and "legalism" continues, there is the need for a continuing and continuous, prayerful study of the Bible. Surely God's will with respect to His plan for the salvation of the human race can be known through the revelation found in the sacred Scriptures. After all, the central theme of the Bible is the salvation and restoration of mankind.

Considering what characterizes much of our society today—hostility toward authority and the attendant war against law and order, denial of responsibility and account-ability because all are "victims" in one way or another, values based upon immediate feeling rather than the ultimate conse-quences of actions, and indulgence and permissiveness disguised as love—we need divine providence to keep us from being influenced by the attitudes that surround us. Moreover, we need to make sure that worldly attitudes don't influence our emphasis and understanding of the doctrine of salvation.

On the other hand, we must be open to changes that are prompted and motivated by our better understanding of the revelation God has given in His Word. God forbid that we should quit studying because we think we have "the truth" or that we need not change what needs to be changed because we already know it all. There is no sin more subtle than that of self-righteousness. But God's grace is constant, fulfilling our every need according to His Word. It is our understanding of that Word through the ministry of the Holy Spirit that I believe will bring us into a unity of faith. To this end I hope and pray that this book may be helpful.

Reconciliation

1

Alienation

She is looking at a tree that fascinates her. It fascinates her not just because of its beauty or uniqueness but because she has been forbidden to eat of its fruit.

Suddenly she hears a voice. It is coming from a very attractive creature, a serpent.

"Didn't God say you shall not eat of any of the trees in this garden?"

"No," she says, "God said we could eat of all the trees of the garden except this one, lest we die. Actually, we're not even supposed to touch this one."

"No, you won't die. God knows that when you eat of it your eyes will be opened and you will be like God, knowing good and evil" (see Gen. 3:1-7).

You know the rest of the story, don't you? She ate and gave some to her husband, and he ate. And immediately things changed, but not for the better. Where was the wisdom? They were miserable because they realized they had lost something very special. They were "naked."

Eating some fruit from a tree. What was so wrong with that? We know the answer to that too, don't we? But let's get the whole picture. We may see something we hadn't noticed before. Let's begin at the beginning:

God

"In the beginning God created the heavens and the earth" (Gen. 1:1). God is a creator God. That says something about

His power, but what about His character?

To begin with, He created an environment that was life-friendly—light, air, water, land. Then he created life—plants, animals, fish, and birds, and the crowning act of creation, Adam and Eve.

But He did not only create life—what we might call "existence." He created the "good life." "And God saw everything that he had made, and behold, it was very good" (v. 31). This being true, we could say that God is pro-life, but because of today's political connotations of that term, we will say He is "life-affirming." And, thus, with respect to His character we know that He is love, because love always seeks to affirm life.

Adam and Eve

We have said that Adam and Eve were the crowning act of God's creation. Why? Because He created them "in His own image" (v. 27).

How special was that?

1. They were created with a high degree of intelligence. They possessed speech communication skills such that God could communicate with them (v. 28), instructing them in His will and purpose for them, to which they could respond with understanding and appreciation, making a meaningful relationship and worship possible. Because they had such intelligence, God could give them significant responsibility. Though God had dominion over all the universe, He gave Adam and Eve subordinate dominion or rulership over all the earth (vv. 26, 28).

2. They were to "be fruitful and multiply" (v. 28) and thus share in God's passion for life. With their intellectual and rational powers they could engage in reproduction intentionally. While the other creatures God made possessed the drive to reproduce, they did not possess the capacity to appreciate

the gift, the joy of sharing in God's power to create human life.

Moral Responsibility

"And the Lord God commanded the man, saying, 'You may freely eat of every tree of the garden; but of the tree of the knowledge of good and evil you shall not eat, for in the day that you eat of it you shall die'" (Gen. 2:16, 17).

From the start, Adam and Eve needed to know that actions are followed by consequences: consequences that are life-affirming and therefore good, and consequences that are life-denying and therefore evil. Through experience, they might have learned what acts are followed by consequences that are life-affirming, but they could "learn" nothing from an act that is followed by a consequence that is life-denying because, obviously, the consequence is death. In either case, they could know nothing of eternal consequences, for such is known only to God. Thus, it was imperative that they heed God's instruction and obey His commandments, not only when He said "yes" but also when He said "no."

Moreover, Lucifer, having been cast out of heaven down to the earth (Rev. 12:9), would certainly tempt Adam and Eve to join him in his rebellion, challenging God's knowledge and authority with respect to consequences. But that should not have been too great a temptation, for they were children of a father-God who is life-affirming so that even when He says "no" He is saying "yes" to life.

For instance, when a mother tells her son that he must not jump into the deep water or he will drown, she is informing him of an action with a consequence that is life-denying. She is giving him a rule or law to follow that is critical to his survival. Because she loves him, her "no" is a "yes" to life.

Freedom to Choose

It is clear from the test concerning the forbidden tree that Adam and Eve were given the freedom to make moral choices. They could either obey God's commandment and do what is right or good, or they could disobey God and do what is wrong or evil. Had they been given no choice in this matter, but rather been predetermined to follow the "sovereign will of God," the test would have been pointless. Clearly, freedom to choose either to obey or disobey God was granted. Death was a very real possibility.

For this reason, God did not, in the beginning, give Adam and Eve inherent immortality (which removes the possibility of death). With the freedom to disobey, they and their offspring could bring disaster to God's creation. That is why He provided the test. Should they keep God's commandment, giving God the assurance that they would be faithful in choosing to obey Him, life was assured. They had access to the Tree of Life.

The Fall

Unfortunately, tragically for us all, they failed the test.

Why, oh why, oh why did they do it? It was not just good food, the delight to the eyes, and wisdom that tempted them. They had those things already—they lived in Eden where every prospect was pleasing, and they were of superior intelligence. What they fell for was the possibility of being *God* rather than the *image of God*. Being like God, "knowing good and evil"—knowing not only immediate and ultimate consequences but eternal consequences as well—they would have to take orders from no one. If such "freedom" could be had through disobedience, then disobedience was a good thing. But it was not just a question of rejecting God's authority. It was a matter of *assuming* God's authority.

The Consequences

That was the act. These were the consequences:

1. A broken relationship with God. "And they heard the sound of the Lord God walking in the garden in the cool of the day, and the man and his wife hid themselves from the presence of the Lord God among the trees of the garden" (Gen. 3:8).

"But the Lord God called to the man, and said to him, 'Where are you?'" (v. 9). This passage must not be passed over. It does not speak of a consequence but calls for a priceless commentary on the character of God. He should have been indignant. He should have wiped them from the face of the earth. To assume God's authority—what presumption and ingratitude! But He went looking for them. That is why He has been called "the hound of heaven." We may be alienated from Him, but He still comes looking for us. "O the depth of the riches and wisdom and knowledge of God! How unsearchable are his judgments and how inscrutable his ways!" (Rom. 11:33).

2. The beginning of a relationship of fear. "And he (Adam) said, 'I heard the sound of thee in the garden, and I was afraid, because I was naked; and I hid myself'" (Gen. 3:10). They could have said, "Yes, we're sorry. We don't deserve your love or your compassion. Do with us what you must." Perhaps that is what God was looking for. But no. That was not to be. Character had already been damaged.

3. Assuming God's authority not only brought alienation between God and Adam and Eve, but affected the relationship between Adam and Eve as well. "The man said, 'The woman whom thou gavest to be with me, she gave me fruit of the tree, and I ate.' Then the Lord God said to the woman, 'What is this that you have done?' The woman said, 'The serpent beguiled me and I ate'" (v. 12, 13).

4. The full joy of sharing in the power to create human life was gone. "To the woman he said, 'I will greatly multiply your pain in childbearing; in pain you shall bring forth children, yet your desire shall be for your husband, and he shall rule over you'" (Gen. 3:16). Life as they had known it was lost. "In the day that you eat of it you shall die."

5. Adam and Eve and their offspring were depraved in character. Their first child, Cain, murdered his brother. And from that day to this, the record is clear: ". . . *all have sinned* and fall short of the glory of God" (Rom. 3:23).

6. They would return to the ground from which they had been formed. "And to Adam he said, 'Because you have listened to the voice of your wife, and have eaten of the tree of which I commanded you, 'You shall not eat of it,' cursed is the ground because of you; in toil you shall eat of it all the days of your life; thorns and thistles it shall bring forth to you; and you shall eat the plants of the field. In the sweat of your face you shall eat bread till you return to the ground, for out of it you were taken; you are dust, and to dust you shall return'" (vv. 17-19).

7. The door to a "forever life" was closed. "'Behold, the man has become like one of us, knowing good and evil; and now, lest he put forth his hand and take also of the tree of life, and eat, and live for ever'—therefore the Lord God sent him forth from the garden of Eden, to till the ground from which he was taken. He drove out the man; and at the east of the garden of Eden he placed the cherubim, and a flaming sword which turned every way, to guard the way to the tree of life" (vv. 22-24).

Could It Have Been Otherwise?

What a tragic end to what had been such a glorious beginning! But could it have been otherwise? Had they

acknowledged their sin and promised never again to disobey
Him, couldn't a God of love have restored them to Edenic
perfection? Couldn't He have given them another chance?

Given our popular concept of permissive, gratuitous love,
the question seems appropriate. But God's love is not that
frivolous or irresponsible. Immediate restoration under the
circumstances was not that simple for the following reasons:

1. What assurance or satisfaction could Adam and Eve
give that their promise would be kept for eternity—world
without end? As created beings who had failed and fallen,
could they provide the assurance of continuous, eternal
obedience, either for themselves or for their offspring? Should
their promise be kept for a million years (when eternity
would have just begun), another fall would precipitate the
crisis all over again.

2. How often is God prepared to disregard the law of
cause and effect, of consequences that follow actions, in
order to forgive sin because of the sinner's promise not to do
it again? To do so is to perpetuate evil, which in turn guaran-
tees ultimate extinction. No. It is because He is love that God
cannot allow behavior that would seem to affirm life immediately but deny life ultimately or eternally. The future of the
entire universe is at stake. When God says "no" He is saying
"yes" to life. Unconditional forgiveness is impossible.
Assurance or satisfaction must be given that rebellion will not
arise again.

God's Grace

What God said to Adam and Eve after the Fall was bad
news indeed. All seemed lost. But what He said to the serpent
(identified as the Devil and Satan in Rev. 20:2) contained
some wonderfully good news. Not for Satan, to be sure, but
for all of us. "I will put enmity between you and the woman,

and between your seed and her seed; he shall bruise your head, and you shall bruise his heal" (Gen. 3:15).

And why was that good news?

1. There is to be enmity between Satan and the woman. Humanity was not to be *totally* depraved. Paul clarifies this by writing of his own experience in Romans 7: "We know that the law is spiritual; but I am carnal, sold under sin. I do not understand my own actions. For I do not do what I want, but I do the very thing I hate. . . . For I know that nothing good dwells within me, that is in my flesh. *I can will what is right, but I cannot do it"* (vv. 14, 15, 18).

It is clear, the human race has been morally depraved, and that depravity centers in the *lack of power to obey.* While the offspring of Adam and Eve cannot *do* what is right, they can *will* or *want* to do it. This is why, prompted and encouraged by the Holy Spirit, they can respond to the call and invitation of God for salvation. They are free to choose the Saviour and reject the Serpent, or choose the Serpent and reject the Saviour. And this is why they are held accountable for the choice they make.

There are people of every race and nation throughout the world who have a desire to do what is right. They are morally conscientious. But, like all of us, without Christ they lack the knowledge and power to always act in a life-affirming way. Unfortunately, the road to hell can be filled with good intentions.

Again, we may presume it could have been otherwise. Couldn't God have solved the sin problem by changing the nature of Adam and Eve, denying them the freedom of choice? But would that solution be worth the cost? First of all, it would deprive Adam and Eve of experiencing a love relationship. They could not really love each other, nor could they have a love relationship with God, because love requires freedom.

For instance, would you love your spouse if your relationship with one another were devoid of choice? Wives, would you love your husband if you knew he brought you a bouquet of roses because he had to rather than because he chose to? Husbands, would you love your wife if you knew she kissed you because she had to rather than because she chose to? So it is with God. Can we say that we love Him if we cannot choose to do so? How can a creature made in "the image of God" be denied the capacity to love if God is love?

Moreover, taking from Adam and Eve the freedom of choice would be an admission that the original creation was a mistake, that the creation of free moral agency and the eternal security of the universe are incompatible. But God was not prepared to make that admission. There was a way to preserve freedom of choice, and hence the image of God in mankind, and at the same time guarantee the eternal security of the universe. And that way is the way of salvation, God's plan to redeem what was lost.

2. "He," a seed of the woman, would triumph over Satan. This was the promise of a Saviour. By God's grace, the "fall" engineered by the serpent would be overcome. This was good news! This *is* good news! This is what the plan of salvation is all about. This is what the Bible is all about—the revelation of God's ultimate purpose for His creation.

When God created mankind, He ran a great risk, and He knew it. There was the possibility that the creature made in His image would choose to disobey or rebel against Him. In anticipation of this possibility, God set forth a plan as revealed in 1 Pet. 1:18-20: "You know that you were ransomed from the futile ways inherited from your fathers, not with perishable things such as silver and gold, but with the precious blood of Christ, like that of a lamb without blemish or spot. He was destined *before the foundation of the world* but was made manifest at the end of the times for your sake." The plan of salvation was not an afterthought. According to Paul, this is "the mystery hidden for ages in God who created all things; that through the church the manifold wisdom of God might now be made known. . . . This was according to the eternal purpose which he has realized in Christ Jesus our Lord . . ." (Eph. 3:9-11).

That "the manifold wisdom of God might now be made known" is a promise and a challenge. We are challenged to seek that wisdom and to share it with one another. It is this challenge that produces books like this.

2

Reconciliation

We are watching three men being tortured to death. It is an execution unspeakably cruel and savage—a crucifixion.

So why are we watching?

Because of the man nailed to the center cross. He has always been so good and kind, a miracle worker. He fed the hungry, comforted the distressed, healed the sick, raised the dead. But He was a heretic whose teachings threatened the religious orthodoxy and political security of the Jewish establishment. He had to go.

What holds our interest at present, however, are His words from the cross: "Father, forgive them; they know not what they do"—words of love and compassion. "My God, my God, why hast thou forsaken me?"—words of rejection and despair. "Father, into thy hands I commit my spirit!"—words of surrender and commitment. And finally, as He breathes His last, "It is finished." [1]

It is finished! What does that mean? To those who love Him it is good news; His suffering is at an end. To those who hate Him it is good news; they will be rid of Him. But what does it mean to you and me, and to all who have "believed" from then until now?

It is more than just good news. It is the gospel! "In Christ God was reconciling the world to himself" (2 Cor. 5:19). Jesus' mission of reconciliation was finished.

Throughout the Old Testament, the promise of a Saviour is cherished as a blessed hope. We hear echoes of it in the words of Jacob: "The scepter shall not depart from Judah, nor the ruler's staff from between his feet, until he comes to whom it belongs; and to him shall be the obedience of the peoples" (Gen. 49:10). In the words of Balaam: "I see him, but not now; I behold him, but not nigh: a star shall come forth out of Jacob, and a scepter shall rise out of Israel" (Num. 24:17). In the words of Moses: "The Lord your God will raise up for you a prophet like me from among you, from your brethren—him you shall heed—just as you desired of the Lord your God at Horeb" (Deut. 18:15, 16). And in the words of Isaiah: "For to us a child is born, to us a son is given; and the government will be upon his shoulder, and his name will be called 'Wonderful Counselor, Mighty God, Everlasting Father, Prince of Peace.' Of the increase of his government and of peace there will be no end, upon the throne of David, and over his kingdom, to establish it, and to uphold it with justice and with righteousness from this time forth and for evermore. The zeal of the Lord of hosts will do this" (Isa. 9:6, 7).

Then it happened. In the days of Herod the king of Judea, an angel of the Lord appeared to Joseph in a dream and said, "Joseph, son of David, do not fear to take Mary your wife, for that which is conceived in her is of the Holy Spirit; she will bear a son, and you shall call his name Jesus, for he will save his people from their sins" (Matt. 1:20, 21). "And when the time had fully come, God sent forth his Son, born of a woman, born under the law, to redeem those who were under the law" (Gal. 4:4).

Jesus, the Messiah, the promised seed of Genesis 3:15, was born of a woman, and the witness to Christ's humanity is clear: *"Since therefore the children share in flesh and blood, he himself likewise partook of the same nature. . . .* For surely it is not with angels that he is concerned but with the descendants of Abraham. Therefore he had to be made like his brethren in every respect . . ." (Heb. 2:14-17). "Have this mind among yourselves, which is yours in Christ Jesus, who, though he was in the form of God, did not count equality with God a thing to be grasped, but emptied himself, taking the form of a servant, being born in the likeness of men" (Phil. 2:5-7). In his humanity He was like us. Either He was Mary's son or God has perpetrated a tremendous hoax. If He was not Mary's son, God should have created Him from the dust as he did Adam and brought Him to His mission fully grown.

Being the son of Mary, he inherited a humanity that had suffered the consequences of Adam's sin for thousands of years. Yet He was not a sinner. I do not believe that the idea of inherited guilt is taught in the Bible, as presumed in the doctrine of the immaculate conception, which frees Mary from inherited guilt so that her son could be born sinless. However, the Bible does teach, as already indicated, that the whole human race suffers the consequences of the original sin.

Christ could be tempted. "For because he himself has suffered and been tempted, he is able to help those who are tempted" (Heb. 2:18). But being tempted, He did not sin. "For we have not a high priest who is unable to sympathize with our weaknesses, but one who in every respect has been tempted as we are, yet without sin" (Heb. 4:15). What this says is that in His humanity He was attracted by that which God had forbidden, yet He never yielded. *He never acquired a propensity to sin by sinning.* That is an important distinction in Christ's humanity: He did not sin. "He committed no sin; no guile was found on his lips" (1 Pet. 2:22).

Another distinction is found in the fact that He was born of the Holy Spirit. "And the angel said to her, 'Do not be afraid, Mary, for you have found favor with God. And behold, you will conceive in your womb and bear a son, and you will call his name Jesus.' . . . And Mary said to the angel, 'How shall this be, since I have no husband?' And the angel said to her, 'The Holy Spirit will come upon you, and the power of the Most High will overshadow you; therefore the child to be born will be called holy, the Son of God'" (Luke 1:30, 31, 34, 35).

So Christ was fully human, but He was also divine, and that divinity is never questioned in Scripture. "In the beginning was the Word, and the Word was with God, and the Word was God. He was in the beginning with God; all things were made through him, and without him was not anything made that was made" (John 1:1-3). "In many and various ways God spoke of old to our fathers by the prophets; but in these last days he has spoken to us by a Son, whom he appointed the heir of all things, through whom also he created the world. He reflects the glory of God and bears the very stamp of his nature, upholding the universe by his word of power" (Heb. 1:1-3). "He is the image of the invisible God, the first-born of all creation; for in him all things were created. . . . He is before all things, and in him all things hold together. . . . For in him *all the fullness of God* was pleased to dwell . . ." (Col. 1:15-17, 19).

How are we to understand all this? In its fullness, we can't, of course. It was a mystery to Paul (1 Tim. 3:16). It will always remain a mystery to us. We must not deny Christ's humanity, but neither must we deny His divinity. Jesus was unique, the "only begotten" Son of God.

He was like us but different. He was born of the Holy Spirit at birth; we are not. We are "born of the Spirit" when we accept Him as our personal Saviour and Lord. He was born of the Spirit at birth so that, in His humanity as a child

of Mary, He might not only have the will to obey, but the
power as well. Thus he could be tested and tried as Adam
was, with the possibility of succeeding where Adam failed.

He Did It

How He succeeded and what that means in terms of our
salvation is at the heart of our study. Note with care the
following passages from Scripture:

"Although he was a Son, *he learned obedience through
what he suffered;* and being made perfect he became the
source of eternal salvation to all who obey him . . ." (Heb.
5:8, 9). "And being found in human form he humbled himself
and became *obedient unto death,* even death on a cross.
Therefore God has highly exalted him and bestowed on him
the name which is above every name, that at the name of
Jesus every knee should bow, in heaven and on earth and
under the earth, and every tongue confess that Jesus Christ is
Lord, to the glory of God the Father" (Phil. 2:8-11).

In Romans, Paul speaks of, ". . . Adam, who was a type
of the one who was to come." The meaning of this he spells
out in some detail, clearly identifying "the one who was to
come." "For if many died through one man's trespass, much
more have the grace of God and the free gift in the grace of
that one man Jesus Christ abounded for many. . . . If, because
of one man's trespass, death reigned through that one man,
much more will those who receive that abundance of grace
and the free gift of righteousness reign in life through the one
man Jesus Christ.

"Then as one man's trespass led to condemnation for all
men, so one man's act of righteousness leads to acquittal and
life for all men. For as by *one man's disobedience many were
made sinners, so by one man's obedience many will be made
righteous"* (Rom. 5:14, 15, 17-19).

Why Jesus, as the second Adam, can be our Saviour is more clearly revealed through a word found in Romans 3:24, 25: "They are justified by his grace as a gift, through the redemption which is in Christ Jesus, whom God put forward as an *expiation* by his blood, to be received by faith." The word in the original Greek which here is translated "expiation" is *hilasterion*. But what does it mean?

According to *The New Analytical Greek Lexicon, hilasterion* means "the cover of the ark of the covenant, the mercy seat." How this is to be understood is clarified in the verb form of the word, *hilaskomai,* which means "to expiate, make an atonement." In the passage quoted above, the King James Version translates *hilasterion* by the word "propitiation," and the New International Version has it "a sacrifice of atonement." What do these words mean? According to *Webster's Ninth New Collegiate Dictionary,* "expiation" means "the act of making atonement"; "propitiation" means "something that regains favor: an atoning sacrifice"; and "atonement" means "reconciliation or reparation for an offense or injury: satisfaction."

At the risk of over-simplification (trying to make the language more clear and less ambiguous), it would seem that the word "satisfaction" is a common denominator. Expiation, propitiation, and atonement provide *satisfaction.*

But what did Jesus satisfy?

1. He satisfied God's wrath against the violation of the laws of life, the consequence or "wages" of which is death— the denial of life. A life-affirming God is angered by behavior that is life-denying; it is unacceptable. Having said this, we must avoid portraying God as inherently vindictive or vengeful. Alienation on God's part was not animosity born of a wounded pride. He did not hate those whom He had created in love. He loved them. But sin alienates; it comes

between God and the sinner. "Your iniquities have made a separation between you and your God, and your sins have hid his face from you so that he does not hear" (Isa. 59:2).

2. He satisfied God's justice. A life-affirming God is not willing that the whole universe should suffer the consequences of life-denying behavior. He cannot affirm the life of creatures made in His image who find pleasure in rebelling against His life-affirming law.

3. In His life, He did succeed where Adam and Eve failed. "For as by one man's disobedience many were made sinners, so by one man's obedience many will be made righteous" (as quoted above). His whole life was a life of obedience even unto the shedding of His blood in death. Thus, He provided the satisfaction that Adam and Eve could not give, the *assurance or satisfaction that those who belong to Him will never rebel against God and in due course will be given immortality.* Only thus could God ever be justified in restoring mankind to the Edenic ideal.

In His death "He paid the price for our redemption." As a member of the human race He died, even though He didn't deserve it, fulfilling the consequences of the original sin for all mankind. "And he is the expiation *(hilasmos,* the noun form of *hilaskomai)* for our sins, and not for ours only but also for the sins of the whole world" (1 John 2:2).

Through God's initiative, not ours, the whole world stands in a renewed relationship before Him. Through Christ's atonement, every child of Adam and Eve has the potential to be reconciled to God, since He has reconciled the world to Himself. "For our sake he made him to be sin who knew no sin, so that in him we might become the righteousness of God" (2 Cor. 5:21).

Do we appreciate as we should what all this says about God? As intelligent beings we seek to understand God's plan of redemption as He has revealed it. He has invited us to do so. But God forbid that we should ever take it for granted. God is love because the way He deals with the sin problem produces ultimate and eternal consequences—life and survival for the entire universe.

Incarnation—that one person of the Godhead should become human—staggers the imagination. For the Creator to become the creature can be understood, as someone has suggested, only by a very frail analogy at best: We say sometimes rather silly things like, "You know, my dog understands every word I say!" Really? If that were true, either the dog has risen to your level of intelligence or yours is no higher than his. What would have to happen if you were to live at the level of a dog or a flea? Right, you would have to become a dog or a flea. You begin to get the picture, don't you? God became a man!

Note the contrast between Adam and Eve's presumption in *assuming the authority of God,* and Christ's disposition with respect to equality with God: ". . . who, though he was in the form of God, *did not count equality with God a thing to be grasped,* but emptied himself, taking the form of a servant, being born in the likeness of men. And being found in human form he humbled himself and became obedient unto death, even death on a cross" (Phil. 2:6-8).

There is good reason why the cross is a cherished symbol for Christians. It is a symbol of the sacrifice Christ made for our salvation. He was God. He was the person of the Godhead that created all things in the beginning. He laid aside all the glory, the power, the majesty, the prerogatives of divinity and became a man. In providing the *assurance or satisfaction that makes redemption possible,* He lived a sinless life in the face of severe temptation beyond our comprehension.

We cannot fathom the revulsion that must have welled up within Christ as He was bound by chains, spat upon, and tried in mockery. Through the power of His divinity, one look would have eliminated His adversaries. He was abused, ridiculed, and scorned by the vilest of adversaries. But the crowning act of atonement was His obedience unto death. Why? Because He didn't deserve it. Having lived a sinless life, He didn't deserve death. But His willingness to obey even when it wasn't fair bespeaks a faithfulness and holiness that even Satan cannot challenge.

One day, while driving along the road in India, I saw something I had heard of but had never seen. A man was standing on the shoulder of the road in dust an inch deep (it was the dry season of the year). With arms and hands raised toward heaven he would fall face forward into the dust, bring his knees and legs up under him, then stand up and start the exercise all over again. He was measuring his length along the road. You can imagine what he looked like, body covered with sweat and dust. I stopped and watched for a moment with others who had gathered around him. Then I asked someone near me, "Where is he going?" They said, "Hardwar." Hardwar? I had driven through Hardwar, a place where pilgrims go to bathe in the sacred waters of the Ganges River, but I had driven thirty miles since. Thirty miles! This poor man is measuring his length along the road for thirty miles! Then I asked the next question, "Where did he come from?" "Lucknow." Lucknow!? Lucknow was more than a hundred miles in the other direction. *Well,* I thought, *thank God he's almost there!* It was unreal, more than I could fathom or comprehend.

After a few minutes I continued my journey. As I drove along, one question haunted me: *Why? Why? Why?* I knew why. He was doing what he believed he needed to do to win

God's favor. He had a family that he needed to feed and clothe and house. He hoped to escape pestilence, famine, and flood. For children, he wanted boys rather than girls because for girls he had to provide dowry when they got married, and that could break him financially. Perhaps through this pilgrimage he could attract God's attention and His providence.

As these thoughts coursed through my mind, tears filled my eyes. *No. No!* He doesn't need to do that. He doesn't need to win God's favor—He already has it! That was all settled at the cross. God's initiative has already reconciled us to Himself. No measuring our length along the road, no lying on a bed of nails, no walking through coals of fire, no climbing up stairs on our knees, no saying countless "Hail Marys" or "Our Fathers," no giving of offerings, no penance of any kind.

He did it! Thank God, He did it! He died the death that we deserve in order that we may have the life that He deserved. His final words from the cross were not words of despair and loss. They were words of triumph and victory. "It is finished." God had reconciled the world unto Himself.

3

Justification

We return again to 2 Corinthians 5: "All this is from God, who through Christ reconciled us to himself . . . that is, in Christ God was reconciling the world to himself. . . . We beseech you on behalf of Christ, be reconciled to God" (vv. 18-20).

In the previous reference to this passage we noted that God took the initiative in effecting a reconciliation between Himself and the world, removing the alienation caused by the original sin. In verse 20, however, we note an added dimension, the human response, "be reconciled to God." This is the gospel scenario so fundamental to the doctrine of salvation— the divine initiative followed by the human response. It never changes. The scenario remains the same.

But what is the human response? How are we to be reconciled to God? To begin with, we turn to Romans 5:8-10, where Paul mentions a gift that follows reconciliation not yet considered: "But God shows his love for us in that while we were yet sinners Christ died for us. Since, therefore, we are now *justified* by his blood, much more shall we be saved by him from the wrath of God. For if while we were enemies we were *reconciled* to God by the death of his Son, much more, now that we are reconciled, shall we be saved by his life" (5:8-10).

Notice the close relationship between the words "justified" and "reconciled." While it says that we were reconciled by Christ's death, it also says that we are justified by His blood. In other words, when Christ provided the assurance or satisfaction that made our salvation possible, justification was also made possible. But what does it mean to be "justified"? It means "to be made right" *(dikaiothentes,* from *dikaio-o).*

With that in mind, we turn to Romans 3:21-26 for clarification with respect to the human response to God's initiative. "But now the righteousness of God has been manifested apart from law, although the law and the prophets bear witness to it, the righteousness of God *through faith in Jesus Christ* for all *who believe.* For there is no distinction; since all have sinned and fall short of the glory of God, they are justified *by his grace as a gift,* through redemption which is in Christ Jesus, whom God put forward as an expiation by his blood, *to be received by faith.* This was to show God's righteousness, because in his divine forbearance he had passed over former sins; it was to prove at the present time that he himself is righteous and that he justifies him *who has faith in Jesus."*

Observe how this passage clearly reveals the divine initiative: 1. God put Jesus Christ forward as an expiation by His blood. 2. He provides justification for all by His grace as a gift, for all have sinned and fall short of the glory of God. 3. In His forbearance He passed over former sins. 4. What God has done proves and manifests His righteousness.

Then notice how the passage also clearly reveals the human response: 1. The righteousness of God through faith in Jesus Christ for all who believe. 2. The expiation which God put forward is to be received by faith. 3. God justifies him who has faith in Jesus.

For All Who Believe

This truth in the words of Jesus, so much loved and cherished by Christians everywhere, bears repeating again and again: "For God so loved the world that *he gave his* only Son, that *whoever believes* in him should not perish but have

eternal life" (John 3:16). Divine initiative—God gave His only
Son. Human response—whoever believes in Him.

"About midnight Paul and Silas were praying and singing
hymns to God, and the prisoners were listening to them, and
suddenly there was a great earthquake, so that the foundations of the prison were shaken; and immediately all the
doors were opened and every one's fetters were unfastened.
When the jailer awoke and saw that the prison doors were
open, he drew his sword and was about to kill himself,
supposing that the prisoners had escaped. But Paul cried with
a loud voice, 'Do not harm yourself, for we are all here.' And
he called for lights and rushed in, and trembling with fear fell
down before Paul and Silas, and brought them out and said,
'Men, what must I do to be saved?' And they said, *Believe in
the Lord Jesus,* and you will be saved, you and your household'" (Acts 16:25-31).

The jailer was desperate. He was terrified, facing certain
death if all the prisoners escaped. His question was not
involved, sophisticated. It was succinct and to the point:
"What must I do to be saved?" And the answer was just as
direct and to the point. This was not a time for long preach-
ments or involved theology. He was offered a choice, simple
but unequivocal: "Believe in the Lord Jesus, and you will be
saved."

This is the gospel—so simple, yet so profound! And
because it is profound, it deserves further consideration and
reflection. What does it mean to believe in Jesus?

Notice how the word "believe" is related to the word
"faith" in Romans 3:21-26 (quoted above): "through faith
(pisteos) in Jesus Christ for all who believe *(pisteuontas)."*
Obviously, "faith" and "believe" are from the same root
(pisteuo). But here the context and usage would suggest that
a saving "belief" is through "faith." Thus, Paul's instruction to

the jailer called for that kind of belief.

"To believe" can presuppose the making of a choice or decision. Confronted with facts or data or experience or whatever, we make a decision or choose to believe.

But biblical faith has added connotations. From a study of Hebrews 11, the great faith chapter, we discover different facets or "faces" of faith. Verse 6 speaks of Enoch's faith in these terms: "And without faith it is impossible to please him. For whoever would draw near to God must *believe that he exists. . . .*" This would indicate that—

1. Saving faith is *relational.* It makes pleasing God and drawing near to Him possible.

2. Saving faith is belief that goes *beyond the evidence.* While there is evidence that supports a rational conclusion that God exists, we all know that God's existence cannot be "proven" by the evidence—the evidence is not coercive. Faith is not blind. It does not ignore the evidence. But it chooses to believe even though the evidence is not coercive.

Hebrews 11 also speaks of the faith of Noah. "By faith Noah, being warned by God concerning events as yet unseen, took heed and constructed an ark for the saving of his household . . ." (v. 7). Faith "takes heed." To take heed means more than just hearing or giving attention to what is said. Here the word "heed" is a translation of a form of the verb *eulabeomai,* which means "to reverence God, to be influenced by pious awe." When Noah heard the Word of God he—out of reverence and being influenced by pious awe—obeyed God. *Saving faith is a "heeding" unto obedience,* a commitment to obey whenever the Word of God gives an instruction, counsel, or command.

Actually, it is impossible to believe in God without such commitment because without it the word "God" loses its meaning. Sovereignty is one of the defining characteristics of

God, and sovereignty presupposes obedience. That is why many who are confronted with the evidence that points to God's existence do not confess a faith in God, for to do so brings with it the obligation to obey Him.

And then there is Abraham. "By faith Abraham obeyed when he was called to go out to a place which he was to receive as an inheritance; and he went out, not knowing where he was to go" (v. 8).

To go out, not knowing where he was to go, is unconditional trust. It is not something we do easily in our relationships one with another. I don't even dare think of what my wife would say if I were to pack up all our belongings and start out on a move across country and, in answer to my wife's query as to where we were going, say, "Honey, I haven't the foggiest idea."

In Romans 3-5 Paul writes eloquently of the doctrine of reconciliation and justification. We find these words in Romans 4:3-5: "For what does the scripture say? 'Abraham *believed* God, and it was reckoned to him as righteousness.' Now to one who works, his wages are not reckoned as a gift but as his due. And to one who does not work but *trusts* him who justifies the ungodly, his *faith* is reckoned as righteousness."

Here the word "trusts" is used along with the words "believed" and "faith." Like "believe" and "faith," the word "trust" is a translation of that same word *pisteuo*. "Trust" says something that "believe" does not say and says something definitive about "faith." Not all versions or translations will use the same wording, but the context calls for some word usage in order to make the meaning clear.

Reading on in Romans 4:18-22: "In hope he believed against hope, that he should become the father of many nations; as he had been told, 'So shall your descendants be.'

He did not weaken in faith when he considered his own body, which was as good as dead because he was about a hundred years old, or when he considered the barrenness of Sarah's womb. *No distrust made him waver concerning the promise of God,* but he grew strong in faith as he gave glory to God, *fully convinced that God was able to do what he had promised.* That is why his faith was 'reckoned to him as righteousness.'" When God told Abraham to go, he went. He didn't know where he was to go but he went anyway. When God told him he would be the father of many nations even though his age and the age of his wife made it humanly impossible, no distrust (or disbelief) made him waver concerning God's promises. He was fully convinced that what God promises He is able to fulfill. *Saving faith is unconditional trust.*

"And the scripture was fulfilled which says, 'Abraham believed God, and it was reckoned to him as righteousness'; and he was called the friend of God" (James 2:23). "So you see that it is men of faith who are the sons of Abraham. And the scripture, foreseeing that God would justify the Gentiles by faith, preached the gospel beforehand to Abraham, saying, 'In you shall all the nations be blessed.' So then, those who are men of faith are blessed with Abraham who had faith" (Gal. 3:6-9).

By faith we are children of Abraham. By faith we are friends of God. By faith we are reconciled to God. By faith we are justified. Even though we are born into this world suffering the consequences of Adam and Eve's transgression, reconciliation and justification are possible because of God's initiative and our response. We are saved by God's grace through our faith.

If faith decides to believe when the evidence is not coercive, if faith makes possible a relationship with God that pleases Him, draws us near to Him, presumes a commitment to obey Him, and trusts Him unconditionally, then faith, like love, requires freedom—the freedom of choice. Faith is an act of the will, a choosing to believe. That is why God reckons it to us as righteousness.

We say, "only believe." What do we mean by that? If we mean it is the only thing we have to do for reconciliation and justification, we speak the truth because no works of law are required. If, on the other hand, we are suggesting that it is easy to do, and involves no struggle, contention, or difficulty whatsoever, we speak not the truth because millions of people find believing in Jesus incredible. To believe that Jesus was the Creator, the Messiah, born of a virgin, that He lived a sinless life and was crucified for our salvation, is considered foolishness.

But we who are Christians, under the wooing of God's Spirit, choose to believe all of it, and this *choosing to believe is the "obedience of faith."* Listen to Paul in that glorious benediction with which he closes his epistle to the Romans: "Now to him who is able to strengthen you according to my gospel and the preaching of Jesus Christ, according to the revelation of the mystery which was kept secret for long ages but is now disclosed and through the prophetic writings is made known to all nations, according to the command of the eternal God, to bring about *the obedience of faith*—to the only wise God be glory for evermore through Jesus Christ! Amen" (16:25-27).

Justification—being made right—is possible because we have been reconciled to God by faith. Justification is a gift we receive because of our faith, but it is just the beginning.

The Riches of God's Grace

Have you ever been overwhelmed by gifts of love? How many and what kind of gifts did it take? The gifts of reconciliation and justification alone are overwhelming, but they are also keys that open the floodgates through which pour the riches of God's grace. God loves to give because He is a God of love. Consider the following and be overwhelmed.

Righteousness:

"For as by one man's disobedience many were made sinners, so by one man's obedience many will be made righteous" (Rom. 5:19). Here the word for "righteous" is *dikaioi* from the same root as the word translated "justified" *(dikaio-o,* see above). To be made "right" or righteous is to be justified. When we are justified we are made righteous. Thus, *justification by faith is righteousness by faith.*

Sanctification:

"But you were washed, you were sanctified, you were justified in the name of the Lord Jesus Christ and in the Spirit of our God" (1 Cor. 6:11). If we are justified, we are sanctified, we are set apart and made holy. The word "sanctified" is *hagiasthate,* a form of the verb *hagiazo,* which means "to set apart or make holy." It is the noun form of this word which is found in 1 Corinthians 1:16: "You shall be holy, for I am holy." We are holy because we have been "washed."

"So also David pronounces a blessing upon the man to whom God reckons righteousness apart from works: 'Blessed are those whose iniquities are forgiven, and *whose sins are covered;* blessed is the man against whom the Lord will not reckon his sin'" (Rom. 4:6-8). Our sins are covered because God will not "reckon" *(logizomai,* "to count") our sins against us. Rather it is righteousness, sanctification, holiness, that is "reckoned" to us. "But the words, 'it was reckoned to him' (Abraham), were written not for his sake alone, but for ours also. It will be reckoned to us who believe in him that raised

from the dead Jesus our Lord, who was put to death for our
trespasses and raised for our justification" (Rom. 4:23-25).
This righteousness, this sanctification is a gift. It is *provisional.*
It is provided for us by the death and resurrection of Jesus
Christ. *We are covered by His righteousness.* "For our sake he
made him to be sin who knew no sin, so that in him we might
become the righteousness of God" (1 Cor. 5:21).

Peace with God:

"Therefore, since we are justified by faith, we have peace
with God through our Lord Jesus Christ" (Rom. 5:1). When we
are made right, the cause for alienation has been removed.
Peace with God is a consequence of justification. *It's what
reconciliation is all about.*

We can walk with Him. We can talk to Him as to a friend.
We can weep with Him and rejoice with Him as we share
with Him our sorrows and our joys. We can go to sleep at
night in full assurance that whether we live or die, we are at
peace with the one who has made us and redeemed us. What
a blessing! What a gift! We turn again to Romans 11:33 and
add verse 36: "O the depth of the riches and wisdom and
knowledge of God! How unsearchable are his judgments and
how inscrutable his ways! . . . For from him and through him
and to him are all things. To him be glory for ever. Amen."

The Holy Spirit:

More will be said concerning the Holy Spirit in the pages
to come. But it must be recognized that a special ministry of
the Holy Spirit is given to us when we are reconciled and
justified. Peter's ministry to Cornelius and the Gentiles in
Caesarea recorded in Acts 10 and 11 shows the significance
of this gift.

In defense of his ministry before his critics in Jerusalem,

Peter said, "As I began to speak, the Holy Spirit fell on them just as on us at the beginning. And I remembered the word of the Lord, how he said, 'John baptized with water, but you shall be baptized with the Holy Spirit.' If then God gave the same *gift* to them as he gave to us when we believed in the Lord Jesus Christ, who was I that I could withstand God? When they heard this they were silenced. And they glorified God, saying, 'Then to the Gentiles also God has granted repentance unto life'" (Acts 11:15-18).

Even more to the point are the words found in Ephesians 1:13: "In him you also, who have heard the word of truth, the gospel of your salvation, and have believed in him, were sealed with the promised Holy Spirit, which is the guarantee of our inheritance until we acquire possession of it, to the praise of his glory."

Children of God:

"But to all who received him, who believed in his name, he gave power to become children of God" (John 1:12).

To be reconciled to God is to become a child of God—a relationship to God that is critical to the biblical doctrine of salvation. It is a relationship made possible because of two wonderful gifts that follow reconciliation: 1. A new nature, or *a radical change in disposition or a turning to God in love and commitment,* and 2. Divine power, or *a radical change in ability to live in keeping with God's will.*

The Bible speaks of the first gift in symbolic and metaphorical terms:

1. Through a new birth: "Truly, truly, I say to you, unless one is born anew, he cannot see the kingdom of God. . . . unless one is born of water and the Spirit, he cannot enter the kingdom of God. That which is born of the flesh is flesh, and that which is born of the Spirit is spirit" (John 3:3, 5, 6). Note

how this corresponds with John 1:12, 13: "But to all who received him, who believed in his name, he gave power to become children of God; *who were born, not of the will of the flesh nor of the will of man, but of God."* We are born again when we are made right.

2. Through death and resurrection: "Do you not know that all of us who have been baptized into Christ Jesus were baptized into his death? We were buried therefore with him by baptism into death, so that as Christ was raised from the dead by the glory of the Father, we too might walk in newness of life" (Rom. 6:3, 4). "I have been crucified with Christ; it is no longer I who live, but Christ who lives in me; and the life I now live in the flesh I live by faith in the Son of God, who loved me and gave himself for me" (Gal. 2:20).

3. Through a new creation: "Therefore, if any one is in Christ, he is a new creation; the old has passed away, behold, the new has come" (2 Cor. 5:17).

4. Through regeneration: "But when the goodness and loving kindness of God our Savior appeared, he saved us, not because of deeds done by us in righteousness, but in virtue of his own mercy, by the washing of regeneration and renewal in the Holy Spirit" (Titus 3:4, 5).

5. Through a change of heart: "For by a single offering he has perfected for all time those who are sanctified. And the Holy Spirit also bears witness to us; for after saying, 'This is the covenant that I will make with them after those days, says the Lord: I will put my laws on their hearts, and write them on their minds,' then he adds, 'I will remember their sins and their misdeeds no more'" (Heb. 10:14-17).

In this life, we become children by birth. We are born into a family. So it is that we become children of God; we are "born anew." When? When we "receive him," and "believe on his name."

When we are reconciled to God we are created anew, resurrected to newness of life, regenerated, given a new heart, and born anew. How is all of this put into one word? Impossible! But we try. We speak of a change of "character," a new "nature," both of which are acceptable—they are used in Scripture—but they have connotations that sometimes complicate matters theologically. That is why I have used "disposition" or a "turning to God in love and commitment." We have a new orientation to God and to His will. We stand in His grace (Rom. 5:2). We seek to serve and obey Him. This is because His laws are written on our hearts (Heb. 8:10, 10:16, see above), and when *His* laws become *our* laws we have a personal, inner inclination to obey them. All who have raised children know how that works. When our children accept our laws as their laws, they find it much easier to obey.

The second gift—*a radical change in ability to live in keeping with God's will*—is spoken of in terms of power. "To all who received him, who believe on his name, he gave *power*" (John 1:12).

At the time of His ascension, just before leaving His disciples, Jesus said, "You shall receive power when the Holy Spirit has come upon you" (Acts 1:8). Paul, at the close of a prayer in behalf of the Ephesian believers says, "Now to him who by the *power at work within us* is able to do more abundantly than all that we ask or think, to him be glory in the church in Christ Jesus to all generations, for ever and ever. Amen" (Eph. 3:20, 21). By way of testimony to the Philippians, Paul makes this dramatic statement: *"I can do all things in him who strengthens me"* (Phil. 4:13). The word "strengthens" in this text does not communicate the full meaning of Paul's witness. In the Greek, the word is *dunamis* from which we derive the word "dynamite." Think of it, "I can do all things in him who *endynamites* me!" Talk about power!

To be sure, we cannot do the will of God without this power. There is no way in which we can generate it by ourselves. It is a gift. "For God did not give us a spirit of timidity but a spirit of power and love and self-control" (2 Tim. 1:7). It is a gift that comes when the Holy Spirit comes upon us (Acts 1:8).

Salvation:

"For by grace you have been saved through faith; and this is not your own doing, *it is the gift of God*—not because of works, lest any man should boast" (Eph. 2:8, 9). The witness is clear, it cannot be denied. This salvation is a *gift* not earned by works.

The context of the passage quoted above (Eph. 2) makes it clear that the reference is to justification. "And you he made alive, when you were dead through the trespasses and sins in which you once walked, following the course of this world, following the prince of the power of the air, the spirit that is now at work in the sons of disobedience. Among these we all once lived in the passions of our flesh, following the desires of body and mind, and so we were by nature children of wrath, like the rest of mankind. But God who is rich in mercy, out of the great love with which he loved us, even when we were dead through our trespasses, made us alive together with Christ (by grace you have been saved), and raised us up with him, and made us sit with him in heavenly places in Christ Jesus, that in the coming ages he might show the immeasurable riches of his grace in kindness toward us in Christ Jesus" (Eph. 2:1-7).

"You *have been* saved." It has been accomplished. It is "by grace . . . it is the *gift* of God." God, who is rich in mercy and great love, made us alive when we were dead through our trespasses, so that in ages to come He might show the immeasurable riches of His grace toward us—the divine initiative. It is *"through faith . . . not because of works."* We accept the gift by faith; we choose to believe—the human response.

What are we saved from? We are saved from slavery to sin, being dead through the trespasses and sins in which we once walked, being children of wrath by nature. From being so wrong we are made right. We are justified.

The question *What are we saved from?* is important to our understanding of the words "saved" and "salvation" and how we use them in point of reference. Note how the context in this passage also makes clear that "have been saved" is in reference to justification. This need for clarification will come into focus again in the pages that follow.

Life:

"And this is the testimony, that God gave us eternal life, and this life is in his Son. He who has the Son has life; and he who has not the Son of God has not life" (1 John 5:11, 12).

If all the riches of God's grace were gathered into one word, that word would be "life," the life that we receive *now* in Christ Jesus. This life is called "eternal life" *(zoen aionion)*. These two words from the Greek are *zoe,* which represents a special, spiritual quality of life (in contrast to *bios),* and from *aion,* which represents a period of time of significant character, or a state of things marking an age or era.[2] The term makes reference to a quality of life rather than its duration. Unless the context indicates otherwise, this Greek expression translated "eternal life" is not synonymous with immortality. We shall examine this more closely later. But the change in quality of life for the child of God who has been reborn is dramatic. It is the difference between "life" and "death."

"And this is eternal life, that they know thee the only true God, and Jesus Christ whom thou hast sent" (John 17:3).

Transformation

4

Transformation

Mary Magdalene, Mary the mother of James, and Salome are going to the tomb on Sunday morning. They have spices with which they plan to anoint the body of Jesus. They don't know quite what they will do because they know a large stone covers the entrance to the tomb, and they don't have the strength or means to remove it. But when they get there they are amazed to see that the stone has been removed. So they go inside, and lo and behold, there is a young man dressed in white sitting on the right side of the grave. And he says to them, "Do not be amazed; you seek Jesus of Nazareth, who was crucified. *He has risen,* he is not here" (Mark 16:6).

What unbelievable good news! Well, not at first. Jesus' followers couldn't believe it. But when later they saw Him and touched Him, they knew it was He, and their lives would never be the same.

Have we "seen" Him and "touched" Him? What difference does it make? How important is the resurrection to our salvation? To Paul it makes all the difference in the world. "If Christ has not been raised, your faith is futile and you are still in your sins. Then those also who have fallen asleep in Christ have perished" (1 Cor. 15:17, 18).

If Christ has not been raised, we are still in our sins. Is all that has been said up to this point concerning reconciliation, justification, and salvation by faith to no avail? It is without the resurrection. "For if while we were enemies we were reconciled to God by the death of his Son, much more, now that we have been reconciled, shall we be saved by his life" (Rom. 5:10). Reconciled by Christ's death, saved by His life. There is more to salvation than reconciliation and justification. That is not to say that the resurrection diminishes the glory of the cross. Quite the contrary. It makes its glory more glorious!

Saved and Being Saved

"For the word of the cross is folly to those who are perishing, but to us who *are being saved* it is the power of God" (1 Cor. 1:18).

It is clear from the context that Paul is writing to those who have been saved. He is writing, "To the church of God which is at Corinth, to those sanctified in Christ Jesus, called to be saints together with all those who in every place call on the name of our Lord Jesus Christ, both their Lord and ours" (v. 2). If they have been saved, why does he say, "to us who are *being saved*"?[3] Is there a difference between "have been saved" and "being saved"?

1 Peter 2:1, 2 raises similar questions: "So put away all malice and all guile and insincerity and envy and all slander. Like newborn babes, long for the pure spiritual milk, that you may *grow up to salvation*."[4] If those to whom Peter is writing are "newborn babes," quite obviously they have been "born again," they are believers and, thus, have been saved. Why, then, does he say "grow up to salvation"? Is there a difference between "have been saved" and "grow up to salvation"? Again, the context is significant: "Therefore gird up your minds, be sober, set your hope fully upon the grace that is coming to you at the revelation of Jesus Christ. As *obedient* children, do not be conformed to the passions of your former ignorance, but as he who called you is holy, be holy your-selves in all your *conduct*; since it is written, 'You shall be *holy*, for I am holy.' . . . You know that *you were ransomed*

from the futile ways inherited from your fathers, not with perishable things such as silver or gold, but with the *precious blood of Christ,* like that of a lamb without blemish or spot. . . . Through him you have confidence in God, who raised him from the dead and gave him glory, so that your faith and hope are in God.

". . . You have been *born anew,* not of perishable seed but of *imperishable,* through the living and abiding word of God" (1:13-16, 18, 19, 21, 23).

Christian Growth

This figure of growth unto salvation is found in numerous passages in the New Testament. "We are to grow up in every way into him who is the head, into Christ" (Eph. 4:15). We are to ". . . grow in grace and the knowledge of our Lord and Savior Jesus Christ" (2 Pet. 3:18). We are to be ". . . conformed to the image of his Son" (Rom. 8:29). We are to come to ". . . mature manhood, to the measure of the stature of the fullness of Christ" (Eph. 4:13). "And we all, with unveiled face, beholding the glory of the Lord, are being changed *(metamorphoumetha)* into his likeness from one degree of glory to another; for this comes from the Lord who is the Spirit" (2 Cor. 3:18).

Notice that the word "changed" in the text just quoted is a translation of a Greek word from which we get our English word "metamorphosis." This same word is used in a dramatic passage found in Romans 12:1, 2: "I appeal to you therefore, brethren, by the mercies of God, to present your bodies as a living sacrifice, holy and acceptable to God, which is your spiritual worship. Do not be conformed to this world but be transformed *(metamorphousthe)* by the renewing of your mind, that you may prove what is the will of God, what is good and acceptable and perfect."

"Transformation" is what "being saved" is all about. "We are to grow up," "grow in grace," "come to maturity," "to the measure of the stature of the fullness of Christ." In all of this, "we are being changed into his likeness, from one degree of glory to another."

Growth in Sanctification and Holiness

Sanctification *attends* reconciliation, as clearly indicated in the previous chapter of this book and in passages such as Hebrews 10:10 ("And by that will we *have been sanctified* through the offering of the body of Jesus Christ once for all") and 1 Corinthians 1:2 (quoted above).

Sanctification also *follows* reconciliation, inherent in Christian growth. "May the God of peace himself sanctify you wholly; and may your spirit and soul and body be kept blameless at the coming of our Lord Jesus Christ" (1 Thess. 5:23); "Husbands, love your wives, as Christ loved the church and gave himself up for her, that he might sanctify her, having cleansed her by the washing of water with the word, that he might present the church to himself in splendor, without spot or wrinkle or any such thing, that she might be holy and without blemish" (Eph. 5:25-27); "Finally, brethren, we beseech and exhort you in the Lord Jesus, that as you learned from us how you ought to live and to please God, just as you are doing, you do so more and more. For you know what instructions we gave you through the Lord. For this is the will of God, your sanctification" (1 Thess. 4:1-3). In this context, sanctification is learning how to live and please God.

Throughout the Bible, and in a special way in the New Testament, God reveals His ideal for His children. We find this in several passages written by Paul, the champion of righteousness by faith. The Bible also provides in abundant measure a revelation of how, by God's grace, we may "grow" in keeping with that ideal, what "being saved" means, and how, without the resurrection of Jesus, there would be no such grace or salvation.

Colossians 3:5-17: "Put to death therefore what is earthly in you: fornication, impurity, passion, evil desire, and covetousness, which is idolatry. On account of these the wrath of God is coming. In these you once walked, when you lived in them. But now put them all away: anger, wrath, malice, slander, and foul talk from your mouth. Do not lie to one another, seeing that you have put off the old nature with its practices and have put on the new nature, which is being renewed in knowledge after the image of its creator. Here there cannot be Greek and Jew, circumcised and uncircumcised, barbarian, Scythian, slave, free man, but Christ is all, and in all.

"Put on then, as God's chosen ones, holy and beloved, compassion, kindness, lowliness, meekness, and patience, forbearing one another and, if one has a complaint against another, forgiving each other; as the Lord has forgiven you, so you also must forgive. And above all these put on love, which binds everything together in perfect harmony. And let the peace of Christ rule in your hearts, to which indeed you were called in the one body. And be thankful. Let the word of Christ dwell in you richly, teach and admonish one another in all wisdom, and sing psalms and hymns and spiritual songs with thankfulness in you hearts to God. And whatever you do, in word or deed, do everything in the name of the Lord Jesus, giving thanks to God the Father through him."

Notice the call for commitment—what we should do: "Put to death. . . ." "Put on. . . ." It is a call found again and again in Paul's epistles. Hear him in an earnest appeal to the church, the body of Christ:

Ephesians 4:1-3, 14, 15: "I therefore, a prisoner of the

Lord, beg you to lead a life worthy of the calling to which you have been called, with all lowliness and meekness, with patience, forbearing one another in love, eager to maintain the unity of the Spirit in the bond of peace. . . . so that we may no longer be children, tossed to and fro and carried about with every wind of doctrine, by the cunning of men, by their craftiness in deceitful wiles. Rather, speaking the truth in love, we are to grow up in every way into him who is the head, into Christ. . . ."

How nice it would be if the life of the Christian, being transformed into the likeness of Christ, were painless! But it is not. It is not "automatic" for those who "have been saved." Because we have had a radical change in disposition and a turning to God in love and commitment, the wrath of Satan is kindled against us. "Finally, be strong in the Lord and in the strength of his might. Put on the whole armor of God, that you may be able to stand against the wiles of the devil. For we are not contending against flesh and blood, but against the principalities, against the powers, against the world rulers of this present darkness, against the spiritual hosts of wickedness in the heavenly places. Therefore take the whole armor of God, that you may be able to withstand in the evil day, and having done all, to stand. Stand therefore, having girded your loins with the truth, and having put on the breastplate of righteousness, and having shod your feet with the equipment of the gospel of peace; besides all these, taking the shield of faith, with which you can quench all the flaming darts of the evil one. And take the helmet of salvation, and the sword of the Spirit, which is the word of God" (Eph. 6:10-17). "Indeed all who desire to live a godly life in Christ will be persecuted" (2 Tim. 3:12).

For Paul, life in Christ was a life of discipline. 1 Corinthians 9:25-27: "Every athlete exercises self-control in all things. They do it to receive a perishable wreath, but we an imperishable. Well, I do not run aimlessly, I do not box as one beating the air; but I pommel my body and subdue it, lest after preaching to others I myself should be disqualified." Salvation is not only a matter of coming to the race, it is also a matter of running in the race.

Concerning Christian discipline, there is a rather lengthy passage in Hebrews that is worthy of careful consideration:

Hebrews 12:1-5, 7-9, 12-14: "Therefore, since we are surrounded by so great a cloud of witnesses, let us also lay aside every weight, and sin which clings so closely, and let us run with perseverance the race that is set before us, looking to Jesus the pioneer and perfecter of our faith, who for the joy that was set before him endured the cross, despising the shame, and is seated at the right hand of the throne of God.

"Consider him who endured from sinners such hostility against himself, so that you may not grow weary or faint-hearted. In your struggle against sin you have not yet resisted to the point of shedding your blood. . . . It is for discipline that you have to endure. God is treating you as sons; for what son is there whom his father does not discipline? If you are left without discipline, in which all have participated, then you are illegitimate children and not sons. Besides this, we have had earthly fathers to discipline us and we respected them. Shall we not much more be subjected to the Father of spirits and live? . . .

"Therefore lift your drooping hands and strengthen your weak knees, and make straight paths for your feet, so that what is lame may not be put out of joint but rather be healed. Strive for peace with all men, and for holiness without which no one will see the Lord."

And in Romans 6:1, 2, 12-14, 16 Paul brings all this into perspective with respect to righteousness by faith:

"What shall we say then? Are we to continue in sin that grace may abound? By no means! How can we who died to sin still live in it? . . .

"Let not sin therefore reign in your mortal bodies, to make you obey their passions. Do not yield your members to sin as instruments of wickedness, but *yield yourselves to God* as men who have been brought from death to life, and your members to God as instruments of righteousness. For sin will have no dominion over you, since you are not under law but under grace. . . .

"Do you not know that if you yield yourselves to any one as obedient slaves, you are slaves of the one whom you obey, either of sin, which leads to death, or of *obedience, which leads to righteousness?*"

The admonition is to "yield yourselves to God." This is something we *choose* to do. If we had not the freedom to choose, how could we "yield ourselves"? It is also clear from the text that this is not something we do just once, but rather it is something we continue doing (the Greek verb indicates continuous action); it is central to Christian living because without yielding to God we cannot obey. It is His Spirit that empowers us, not the law.

Notice the words "obedience that leads to righteousness." We have seen that there is a righteousness by faith, and now we see that there is a righteousness which is the result of obedience.

He Lives

About now I hear someone saying, "I give up. I'll never make it! One of the above texts is challenge enough. All of them together is overwhelming." Debbie felt something like that. She sat across the desk from me with her hands upraised and despair written on her face. "I give up. I can never get it

right. I try so hard, and all I ever hear is, 'You must do more.'
I can't do more. I walk around in a cloud of guilt all the time.
If you can't help me, it's all over!" What can we say to Debbie?

The call to holiness can frighten us. We have all met
Debbie, and at one time or another she is probably us. What
we need is the assurance that because He lives, growth in
holiness is doable. It is the living Christ that gives us the
confidence that we need. This is the truth so beautifully
portrayed in the book of Hebrews.

Hebrews 1:3 tells us that after the cross, "when he had
made purification for our sins, He sat down at the right hand
of the Majesty in high." Why is that important? Because of
what He is doing there. "Now the point in what we are saying
is this: we have such a high priest, one who is seated at the
right hand of the throne of the Majesty in heaven, a minister
in the sanctuary and the true tent which is set up not by man
but by the Lord" (Heb. 8:1, 2). Wonderful! Not only is Christ
at the right hand of God but He is there to minister in our
behalf as *our* high priest.

But *how* He ministers as our high priest is love's answer
to our desperate need: "Since therefore the children share in
flesh and blood, he himself likewise partook of the same
nature, that through death he might destroy him who has the
power of death, that is, the devil." "For because he himself
has suffered and been tempted, he is able to help those who
are tempted" (Heb. 2:14, 18).

Now notice what that means in terms of assurance: "Since
then we have a great high priest who has passed through the
heavens, Jesus the Son of God, let us *hold fast our confession.*
For we have not a high priest who is unable to sympathize
with our weakness, but one who in every respect has been
tempted as we are, yet without sin. Let us then *with confidence* draw near to the *throne of grace,* that we may receive

mercy and find grace to help in time of need" (Heb. 4:14, 16).

Observe how the atonement and the priestly ministry of Christ are brought together in the book of Hebrews. For salvation, come to the cross. For salvation, come to the throne of grace. The doctrine of the sanctuary should not only emphasize judgment in the fulfillment of prophecy but also forgiveness and mercy and grace and confidence and assurance. We need that assurance. Our children growing up in the church need it. Debbie needed it. We all make mistakes. At times we all fail to do what we know we should do. We live in a world in which lawlessness, corruption, and perversion must astonish even the devil, but we must not despair.

Christ is our advocate, and we should never doubt that God will forgive. Jesus said that the divine rule of forgiveness is "seventy times seven" (Matt. 18:22). The promise is ours: "If we confess our sins, he is faithful and just, and will forgive us our sins, and cleanse us from all unrighteousness" (1 John 1:9). We may lose some battles, but in Him we are going to win the war! Why? Because we can be "more than conquerors through him who loved us" (Rom. 8:37). We can experience victory in Christ as we await the second advent of our Lord. Why? Because the tomb is empty!

5

No Law, No Grace, No Salvation

John is being disciplined by the church, which seeks to uphold Christian standards in keeping with God's commandments. He has disregarded their counsel and persisted in his disobedience. In anger he reacts to their action and says, "You're all a bunch of legalists. We're not saved by works; we're saved by grace through faith. You just don't get it, do you?"

There are those in the church who agree with him, and there are those who don't. A heated controversy develops, and here comes the "cheap grace" versus "legalism" polarity. Those who agree with him charge, "Legalism." But those who disagree charge back, "Cheap grace."

For the most part, there is no dispute with respect to how we become Christians or children of God in Christ. It is by grace through faith. That was confirmed in two previous chapters of this book. But how we live as Christians in relationship to the law of God has been discussed, debated, and disputed from the early days of Christianity. And the present generation is no different. This, then, is the issue at the heart of the polarity mentioned above: What is the relationship between the law or commandments of God and a Christian who is "being saved," "growing up to salvation," or being "transformed"?

The Function and Purpose of the Law

In the writings of Paul, the law is referred to in terms of its *function*. "Now it is evident that *no man is justified before God by the law*; for 'He who through faith is righteous shall live'; but *the law does not rest on faith*, for 'He who does them shall live by them.' Christ redeemed us from the *curse of the law . . .*" (Gal. 3:11-13). Or Romans 4:13-15: "The Promise of Abraham and his descendants, that they should inherit the world, *did not come through the law* but through the right-eousness of faith. If it is the adherents of the law who are to be the heirs, faith is null and the promise is void. For the law brings wrath, but *where there is no law there is no transgres-sion*." Why there is no transgression if there is no law is clar-ified in Romans 7:7-12: "What then shall we say? That the law is sin? By no means! *Yet, if it had not been for the law, I should not have known sin*. I should not have known what it is to covet if the law had not said, 'You shall not covet.' But sin, finding opportunity in the commandment, wrought in me all kinds of covetousness. *Apart from the law sin lies dead*. I was once alive apart from the law, but when the commandment came, sin revived and I died; the very commandment which promised life proved to be death to me. For sin, finding opportunity in the commandment, deceived me and by it killed me. So the law is holy, and the commandment is holy and just and good."

The law is holy and just and good, but it cannot save. Its function is to inform us of sin and condemn us when we sin. This is just as true in reference to transformation as it is in reference to justification.

But if there is no transgression where there is no law, and apart from the law sin lies dead, there can be no condemna-tion for sinning. And if there is no sin or condemnation, there is no need of grace. And if no need of grace, no need of salvation and no need of a high priest at the throne of grace.

Well, where does that leave us? Without the law, we don't need a gospel. So, does righteousness by faith need the law?

For the answer we go back to Romans 7, 8, where we begin with confusion but end up with a resolution that is glorious and wonderful. "Do you not know, brethren—for I am speaking to those who know the law—that the law is binding on a person only during his life? Thus a married woman is bound by law to her husband as long as he lives; but if her husband dies she is discharged from the law concerning her husband. Accordingly, she will be called an adulteress if she lives with another man while her husband is alive. But if her husband dies she is free from that law, and if she marries another man she is not an adulteress.

"Likewise, my brethren, you have died to the law through the body of Christ, so that you may belong to another, to him who has been raised from the dead in order that we may bear fruit unto God. While we were living in the flesh, our sinful passions, aroused by the law, were at work in our members to bear fruit for death. But now we are discharged from the law, dead to that which held us captive, so that we serve not under the old written code but in the new life of the Spirit" (Rom. 7:1-6).

There you have it. We are dead to the law, discharged from the law. Thus, we are free from sin and sinning. But wait! It is at this very point that Paul declares the holiness, justice, and goodness of the law and begins to unfold that glorious and wonderful resolution.

"Did that which is good, then, bring death to me? By no means! It was sin, working death in me through what is good, in order that sin might be shown to be sin, and through the commandment might become sinful beyond measure. We know that the law is spiritual; but I am carnal, sold under sin. I do not understand my own actions. For I do not do what I want, but I do the very thing I hate. Now if I do what I do not want, I agree that the law is good. So I find it to be a law that when I want to do right, evil lies close at hand. For I delight in the law of God, in my inmost self, but I see in my members another law at war with the law of my mind and making me captive to the *law of sin* which dwells in my members. Wretched man that I am! Who will deliver me from this body of death? Thanks be to God through Jesus Christ our Lord! So then, I myself serve the *law of God* with my mind, but with my flesh I serve the *law of sin*" (vv. 13-25).

At this point we must stop and call attention to the fact that two laws have been mentioned in the above passage. First, there is the *law of God,* and then there is the *law of sin.* From which law does Paul want to be delivered? Let's read on in Chapter 8:

"There is now no condemnation for those who are *in Christ Jesus.* For *the law of the Spirit of life in Christ Jesus* has set me free from *the law of sin and death.* For God has done what the law, weakened by the flesh, could not do: sending his own Son in the likeness of sinful flesh and for sin, condemned sin in the flesh, in order that *the just requirements of the law might be fulfilled in us,* who walk not according to the flesh but according to the Spirit" (vv. 1-4).

Now isn't that interesting? Not only do we have two laws but now we have a third: "the law of the Spirit of life in Christ Jesus." Isn't it wonderful! The third law frees us from "the law of sin and death."

Notice it says that the just requirements of the law are fulfilled in those who walk according to the Spirit. What does it mean to walk according to the Spirit? Paul tells us in verse five: "For those who live according to the flesh set their minds

on the things of the flesh, but those who live according to the
Spirit set their minds on the things of the Spirit." This we can
do because we have been freed from the law of sin and
death. To be in Christ is to have the freedom to "set our
mind." It is a freedom that Christ provides in keeping with the
freedom of choice that God will not take from us because we
were made in His image. It is that freedom that is so beautifully portrayed in Paul's formula for salvation found in
Philippians 2:12, 13: "Therefore, my beloved, as you have
obeyed, so now, not only as in my presence but much more
in my absence, work out your own salvation with fear and
trembling; for God is at work in you, both to will and to work
for his good pleasure."

Work Out Your Own Salvation:

The first part of the formula is our responsibility. In
choosing to be in Christ, to abide in Him, we are empowered
to walk according to the Spirit. We set our minds on the
things of the Spirit; we work out our own salvation. We put
on the whole armor of God that we may stand against the
wiles of the devil. We gird our loins with truth, we put on the
breastplate of righteousness, we have our feet shod with the
equipment of the gospel of peace, we use the shield of faith
with which all the flaming darts of the evil one can be
quenched, we take the helmet of salvation, and the sword of
the Spirit, which is the word of God. We pray at all times in
the Spirit, with all prayer and supplication (see Eph. 6:10-18,
quoted above).

God Is at Work in Us:

The second part of the formula is God's responsibility.
The empowerment comes from Him. "For all who are led by
the Spirit of God are sons of God. . . . When we cry 'Abba

Father' it is the Spirit himself bearing witness with our spirit that we are children of God, and if children, then heirs, heirs of God and fellow heirs with Christ, provided we suffer with him in order that we may also be glorified with him" (Rom. 8:14-17). While we are doing our part, God is doing His. Or, because God has and is doing His part, we are doing ours.

Let us not deceive ourselves by thinking that when we are in Christ we become robots of the Holy Spirit, that obedience becomes "automatic." I repeat this because of the present-day obsession with the idea that we are not responsible for our actions. It is an idea that can be very attractive and assuring, but Satanic in origin, especially when it provides us with a false "assurance of salvation."

Paul versus James

Many who read and study the Bible are deeply perplexed because Paul and James do not always speak of faith and works in the same way. Why is this? Could it be that they are writing from somewhat different perspectives?

Paul's Perspective:

In Galatians 2 Paul speaks of his calling in defense of his ministry:

"Then after fourteen years I went up again to Jerusalem with Barnabas, taking Titus along with me. I went up by revelation; and laid before them (but privately before those who were of repute)⁵ the gospel which I preached among the Gentiles, lest somehow I should be running or had run in vain. . . .—those, I say, who were of repute added nothing to me; but on the contrary, when they saw that I had been entrusted with the gospel to the uncircumcised, just as Peter had been entrusted with the gospel to the circumcised (for he who worked through Peter for the mission to the circumcised worked through me also for the Gentiles), and when they perceived the grace that was given me, James and Cephas and John, who were reputed to be pillars, gave to me and Barnabas the right hand of fellowship, that we should go to the Gentiles . . ." (Gal. 2:1-9).

But then in Antioch, Paul confronts Peter and charges him with misrepresenting the truth.[6] At issue was the question of circumcision (v. 12) and the keeping of law in order to be children of God. For Paul, circumcision was no longer necessary as a sign that one was a part of God's special people (5:2, 6); justification was by grace through faith.

And so Paul, in writing to the church, often writes from the perspective of an apostle to the Gentiles who were ". . . separated from Christ, alienated from the commonwealth of Israel, and strangers to the covenant of promise, having no hope and without God in the world" (Eph. 2:12). Such were in need of reconciliation and justification and this was made possible only by faith. And thus it would be for all, whether of the circumcision or not, who had not accepted Christ and been reconciled to God. It is with this in mind that he so often speaks of "works." "Then what becomes of our boasting? It is excluded. On what principle? On the principle of works? No, but on the principle of faith. For we hold that a man is justified by faith apart from works of law" (Rom. 3:27, 28). Also Romans 4:2-6: "For if Abraham was justified by works, he has something to boast about, but not before God. For what does the scripture say? 'Abraham believed God, and it was reckoned to him as righteousness.' Now to one who works, his wages are not reckoned as a gift but as his due. And one who does not work but trusts him who justifies the ungodly, his faith is reckoned as righteousness. So also David pronounces a blessing upon the man to whom God reckons righteousness apart from works. . . ." And Romans 9:30-32: "What shall we say, then? That Gentiles who did not pursue righteousness have attained it, that is, righteousness through faith; but that Israel who pursued the righteousness which is based on law did not succeed in fulfilling that law. Why? Because they did not pursue it through faith, but as if it were based on works."

James' Perspective:

James writes as a pastor or ". . . servant of the Lord Jesus Christ, To the twelve tribes in the Dispersion" (James 1:1), who ". . . hold the faith of our Lord Jesus Christ, the Lord of glory" (2:1). From what he writes, his problem is with those who set faith over against works in a radical discontinuity, holding to the belief that salvation is by faith alone devoid of good works at any point in the salvation process, growth in Christ notwithstanding. In rejecting such discontinuity and writing as "a servant of God and of the Lord Jesus Christ" (1:1) and writing about "the faith of our Lord Jesus Christ, the Lord of Glory" (2:1), James says, "What does it profit, my brethren, if a man says he has faith but has not works? Can his faith save him? If a brother or sister is ill-clad and in lack of daily food, and one of you says to them, 'Go in peace, be warmed and filled,' without giving them the things needed for the body, what does it profit? So *faith by itself,* if it has no works, is *dead"* (James 2:14-17).

Note the context; he is not talking about a person coming to Christ in faith to be reconciled to God. He is talking about a "brother" or "sister," which would indicate that he is talking about those who are living in Christ and should be growing up to salvation. "But some will say, 'You have faith and I have works.' Show me your faith apart from your works, and I by my works will show you my faith. You believe that God is one; you do well. Even the demons believe—and shudder. Do you want to be shown, you shallow man, that faith apart from works is barren?" (vv. 18-20). And now, like Paul, he uses Abraham as an example, but notice that his reference to Abraham is different from Paul's. Paul's reference was made with respect to the promise that Abraham would have a son in his old age, which was contrary to nature and, therefore, something he could do nothing about except to believe and trust God. But James' reference to Abraham was made with respect to something God asked him to do after the son was born, which he could do. "Was not Abraham our father justi-fied by works, when he offered his son Isaac upon the altar? You see that *faith was active along with his works,* and *faith was completed by works,* and the scripture was fulfilled which says, 'Abraham believed God, and it was *reckoned to him as righteousness*'; and he was called the friend of God. You see that a man is justified by works and not by faith alone. . . . For as the body apart from the spirit is dead, so faith apart from works is dead" (James 2:21-24, 26). *This faith is a heeding unto obedience* (see in Chapter 3 on the facets of faith in Hebrews 11). Good works are the outgrowth of faith even as transformation is the outgrowth of reconciliation. That is why James can say that we are justified by works (doing what God has instructed us to do) and not by faith alone.

But this, too, is a part of Paul's doctrine of righteousness by faith when there is a need to instruct the believers in living the Christian ideal as it relates to obedience and good works. Remember that at the confrontation in Jerusalem mentioned above, James as one of the men of repute gave him the hand of fellowship. And so Paul speaks of obedience that leads to righteousness (Rom. 6:16) and of "Jesus Christ, who gave himself for us to redeem us from all iniquity and to purify for himself a people of his own who are zealous for *good deeds"* (Titus 2:14), and of how we ". . . are his workmanship, created *in Christ Jesus* for *good works*, which God prepared beforehand, that we should walk in them" (Eph. 2:10). Consider, also, passages from his epistles to the Ephesians and the Colossians quoted in the previous chapter.

While in reconciliation there is a discontinuity between faith and works, in transformation—salvation from a life of disobedience—there is no such discontinuity. Obedience is not "works" done to win God's favor but "good works" which are possible because we already have God's favor.

It is worth noting that in John's portrait of the saints in Revelation 19:7, 8, it says, "Let us rejoice and exult and give him the glory, for the marriage of the Lamb has come, and his Bride has made herself ready; it was granted her to be clothed with fine linen, bright and pure—for the fine linen is the *righteous deeds* of the saints." Righteousness is not only right being; it is also right doing.

When we say, "We are not saved by keeping God's commandments, but we cannot be saved without keeping them," I hope we realize we are using the word "saved" in two different points of reference. The first "saved" is in reference to reconciliation, and the second "saved" in reference to transformation. Without that distinction, the statement is a classic example of doublespeak.

Whether we speak of righteousness as "being" or "doing," it is always "in Christ." Any doing without Christ is "works" because it is without faith. The law does not save us but informs us of our sin, prompting us to "draw near to the throne of grace, that we may receive mercy and find grace in time of need" (Heb. 4:16).

Because there is law, there is sin. Because there is sin, there is grace. And because there is grace, there is salvation.

6

The Christian Way

Since it is clear that without the law there is no transgression, and where there is no transgression there is no need of grace and salvation, what law or commandments define or identify sin for the children of God in Christ? What is the Christian way? Jesus said it is narrow. How narrow is it?

The Law of Christ

First of all, there are the commandments of Jesus. His teachings are filled with moral instruction. Consider the Sermon on the Mount (Matthew 5-7) in which He speaks of so many things we should do in order to be "blessed." Notice also how He affirms the law: "Think not that I have come to abolish the law and the prophets; I have come not to abolish them but to fulfill them. For truly, I say to you, till heaven and earth pass away, not an iota, not a dot, will pass from the law until all is accomplished. Whoever then relaxes one of the least of these commandments and teaches men so, shall be called least in the kingdom of heaven; but he who does them and teaches them shall be called great in the kingdom of heaven. For I tell you, unless your righteousness exceeds that of the scribes and Pharisees, you will never enter the kingdom of heaven" (5:17-20).

Note also how He interprets laws already established, including some of the Ten Commandments: "You have heard that it was said to men of old, 'You shall not kill; and whoever kills shall be liable to judgment.' But I say to you that every one who is angry with his brother shall be liable to judgment; whoever insults his brother shall be liable to the council, and whoever says, 'You fool!' shall be liable to the hell of fire" (vv. 21, 22).

"You have heard that it was said, 'You shall not commit adultery.' But I say to you that every one who looks at a woman lustfully has already committed adultery with her in his heart" (vv. 27, 28).

"You have heard that it was said, 'You shall love your neighbor and hate your enemy.' But I say to you, Love your enemies and pray for those who persecute you, so that you may be sons of your Father who is in heaven; for he makes his sun rise on the evil and on the good, and sends rain on the just and on the unjust" (vv. 43-45).

"You, therefore, must be perfect, as your heavenly Father is perfect" (v. 48).

And toward the end of the sermon: "Not every one who says to me, 'Lord, Lord,' shall enter the kingdom of heaven, but he who does the will of my Father who is in heaven" (7:21).

"And when Jesus finished these sayings, the crowds were astonished at his teaching, for he taught them as one who had authority, and not as a scribe" (v. 28).

The Word of God

"All scripture is inspired by God and profitable for teaching, for reproof, for correction, and for training in right-eousness, that the man of God may be complete, equipped for every good work" (2 Tim. 3:16).

Both Old and New Testaments contain numberless commandments and instruction in the do's and don'ts of Godly behavior. We, of course, cannot mention all of them here, and there is no need to do so for many from the New

Testament were noted previously in reference to growth in sanctification and holiness, and throughout this section of the book which proclaims the good news of Transformation. We note here only a few do's and don'ts selected at random from the epistles:[7] Do's—be subject to lawful authority, respect the kind and gentle and the overbearing, bless, keep lips and tongue from evil and speaking vile, seek peace, love one another, love in deed and in truth. Don'ts—no filthiness, wickedness, unbridled tongues, don't return evil for evil or reviling for reviling, do not murder.

And in Galatians we have a point that has been largely overlooked: As we have seen, there is no stronger rejection of the law as a means of reconciliation and justification than in this epistle. Paul will not allow the law to take the place of Jesus Christ. Never! But after he has eloquently made this point he provides a "check list" of sins which, if we commit, will mean that we are lost: "Now the works of the flesh are plain: fornication, impurity, licentiousness, idolatry, sorcery, enmity, strife, jealousy, anger, selfishness, dissension, party spirit, envy, drunkenness, carousing, and the like. I warn you, as I warned you before, that *those who do such things shall not inherit the kingdom of God"* (Gal. 5:19-21). Then he provides a list of characteristics we will possess if we live by the Spirit: "But the fruit of the Spirit is love, joy, peace, patience, kindness, goodness, faithfulness, gentleness, self-control; against such there is no law" (vv. 22, 23). He then briefly defines this list in terms of behavior: "If we live by the Spirit, let us also walk by the Spirit. Let us have no self-conceit, no provoking of one another, no envy of one another" (vv. 25, 26).

The Ten Commandments
Without a doubt, the Ten Commandments have been the

most universally accepted moral code in the Christian world. Many regard it as the guiding force behind the emergence of western civilization. Most conservative Christians who take the Bible as the Word of God believe that these commandments were first written by God on two tables of stone as recorded in Exodus 24:12 and 32:15, 16.

They are referred to a number of times in the New Testament, including in Jesus' Sermon on the Mount, as referred to above, and in His encounter with the rich young ruler: "Do not commit adultery, Do not kill, Do not steal, Do not bear false witness, Honor your father and mother" (Luke 18:20). (Did He endorse only these because He did not mention them all?) Romans 13:8, 9 mentions four of them in a passage we shall return to a bit later: "Owe no one anything, except to love one another; for he who loves his neighbor has fulfilled the law. The commandments, 'You shall not commit adultery, You shall not kill, You shall not steal, You shall not covet,' and any other commandment, are summed up in this sentence, 'You shall love your neighbor as yourself." James, of course, refers to the Ten Commandments as the law of liberty: "For whoever keeps the whole law but fails in one point has become guilty of all of it. For he who said, 'Do not commit adultery,' said also, 'Do not kill.' If you do not commit adultery but do kill, you have become a transgressor of the law. So speak and so act as those who are judged under the law of liberty" (James 2:10-12).

However, as sacred as the Ten Commandments may be, many Christians are uncomfortable with them because the fourth commandment declares the seventh day of the week to be a holy day. Generally, however, this Sabbath commandment is accepted as long as the first day of the week can be kept as the Sabbath in honor of the resurrection of Christ. When pressed because the commandment names the seventh day as holy, the response is either to consider Monday the first day of the week, making Sunday the seventh, or to fall back on the grace side of the grace-versus-law polarity, or to say that the seventh-day Sabbath is Jewish and ceremonial and therefore nailed to the cross, and because of this every day is holy since we are to worship God every day.

For the Israelites, the Sabbath was also a memorial of the Exodus (Deut. 5:12-15) and written as such by Moses in the Book of the Law, but the seventh day has been the Sabbath from the beginning of this world (Gen. 2:1-3) and has always been a memorial of creation and therefore of universal relevance. We can worship on any day of the week, month, or year but that does not make the day holy. Only God makes holy. We keep holy what He makes holy.

But why did God put the Sabbath commandment in the center of the Ten Commandments? First of all, to enrich our relationship: He with us and we with Him. To set aside one seventh of our time to spend with our life-affirming God in worship and communion is a joy and a high privilege for the human family created in His image. For us, it is also life-affirming because of the quality time it provides for communion and fellowship with family, both generic and congregational in the body of Christ. Surely we are all aware of how critical to our physical and mental health is time management in today's world.

Moreover, He did it for the same reason He put the tree of the knowledge of good and evil in the midst of the Garden of Eden. There is no cosmological reason to keep the seventh day of the week holy other than God's act and His Word in making it holy. Physically, it is just like every other day. The sun comes up in the morning and goes down in the evening; it rains or it shines; it can be cold or hot or wonderfully pleasant; there are fewer daylight hours in the winter than in the summer. The Sabbath commandment, however, is God's signature in His law. It identifies Him as the true God—the Creator—and His authority is thus confirmed. To willfully break the Sabbath or to assume we can change the day is to assume the authority of God as did Adam and Eve in Eden.

The Difference Between Rules and Principles

Perhaps the greatest frustration with "works of law" comes from the feeling that we are called upon to keep too many "rules." Remember, that was Debbie's problem, and it has been a problem for many. There are those who have left the church not because they no longer believe its basic doctrines but because of too much legislation of rules—the do's and the don'ts. They find it hard to harmonize that with righteousness by faith, especially when, in all serious consideration, the rules raise the question "Why?" or "Why not?" Where in the world do all those rules come from? Why are we required to keep rules that may have made sense at one time but make no sense now?

While we may not find the issue a justifiable reason for leaving the church, in all honesty, it is worthy of serious consideration. Where do rules come from? Try this: *A rule is often the definition of a principle in terms of behavior.*

Jesus said, "You shall love the Lord your God with all your heart, and with all your soul, and with all your mind. This is the great and first commandment. And a second is like it, You shall love your neighbor as yourself" (Matt. 22:37-39). Here are two principles stated as commandments. What do they mean, or how are they defined in terms of behavior? "On these two commandments depend all the law and the prophets" (v. 40). Do the law and the prophets define these principles? Remember Paul's statement in Romans 13 quoted above? "The commandments, 'You shall not commit adultery, you shall not kill, You shall not steal, You shall not covet,' and any other commandment, are summed up in this sentence [the principle], 'You shall love your neighbor as yourself'" (v. 9). Thus it is with all of the Ten Commandments.

The first four rules define our love for God in terms of behavior:

1. "You shall have no other Gods before me."
2. "You shall not make for yourself a graven image, or any likeness of anything that is in heaven above, or that is in the earth beneath, or that is in the water under the earth; you shall not bow down to them or serve them."
3. "You shall not take the name of the Lord your God in vain."
4. "Remember the sabbath day to keep it holy. . . . for in six days the Lord made heaven and earth, the sea, and all that is in them, and rested the seventh day; therefore the Lord blessed the sabbath day and hallowed it."

The last six rules define our love for our neighbor in terms of behavior:

5. "Honor your father and your mother."
6. "You shall not kill."
7. "You shall not commit adultery."
8. "You shall not steal."
9. "You shall not bear false witness against your neighbor."
10. "You shall not covet . . . anything that is your neighbor's" (Exodus 20:3-17).

Jesus also said, "If you love me [the principle], you will keep my commandments [the rules]" (John 14:15). So it is, we keep His commandments because we love Him. John put it this way: "He who says 'I know him' but disobeys his commandments is a liar, and the truth is not in him; but whoever keeps his word, in him truly love for God is perfected" (1 John 2:4, 5).

But what do we do when the Bible states principles but does not give us rules that define them? For instance, "Do you not know that your body is a temple of the Holy Spirit within you, which you have of God? You are not your own; you were bought with a price. So glorify God in your body" (1 Cor. 6:19, 20).

How do we glorify God in our body?

"So, whether you eat or drink, or whatever you do, do all to the glory of God" (1 Cor. 10:31).

What shall we eat or drink or do to the glory of God?

Or what do we do when the principle and the rules are given but the rules no longer clearly or meaningfully define the principle?

"Also that women should adorn themselves modestly and sensibly in seemly apparel. Not in braided hair or gold or pearls or costly attire" (1 Tim. 2:9).

What behavior did Paul specifically have in mind? Was braided hair then what it is today? What about silver or diamonds or apparel that is sexually provocative? The principle is modesty in apparel, but what does that mean in terms of behavior today?

"Do not love the world or the things in the world. . . . For all that is in the world, the lust of the flesh and the lust of the eyes and the pride of life, is not of the Father but is of the world" (1 John 2:15, 16).

"Do not love the world" is the principle, but what are the lust of the flesh, the lust of the eyes, and the pride of life in terms of behavior?

It is one thing when the Bible or inspired counsel is specific with respect to rules, but it is quite another when a principle must be defined. When such is the case, we must recognize that *principles are eternal*—they do not change—

but their definition in time and place may not always be the same. At one time it was immodest for a woman to wear a skirt at such a length that her ankle might be exposed. This is no longer true. At one time blood-letting was practiced as a treatment for healing the body. Do we continue the practice today in order to maintain or restore health and thus glorify God in our body? In one place it may be thought worldly or a violation of proper stewardship to own a $200,000 home; in another, because of economic circumstances, it may not.

An example of rules or commandments which applied at one time but are no longer binding are the ceremonial laws of the children of Israel in the Old Testament that either commemorated the exodus from Egypt or were symbolic of the mission and ministry of the coming Messiah. "These are only a shadow of what is to come, but the substance belongs to Christ" (Col. 2:17). But the principle of God's love and providence for His people does not change.

To some, the idea that there are rules that defined principles at one time but are no longer relevant is too dangerous even to suggest. To others, trying to sort it all out is a waste of time. These are "matters of lifestyle" which are not to be considered in a discussion of righteousness by faith. But matters of lifestyle cannot be dismissed in this cursory way because Christian behavior is not characterized by how principles are defined but by the principles themselves. Are not Christians to be reverent, moral, lovable, honest, trustworthy, reliable? But what do these principles mean in terms of behavior? And here we are, right back where we started. They have to be defined. The question remains, how are we to define them with respect to time and place?

Consider the following:

1. *Definition by the individual:* Throughout life, there are

times when we each have to make choices and decisions as to how to act or behave in keeping with Christian principle. And the choices and decisions we make are, first and foremost, a personal matter and our own responsibility. But, remember, He has risen! He is at the throne of grace not to tell us it makes no difference with respect to our salvation or to make our decisions for us but to help us and guide us by His Spirit. "When the Spirit of truth comes, He will guide (*hodegeo*) [not manipulate] you into all the truth" (John 16:13).

2. *Definition by the community:* We are all part of a community—a family, a church, a nation. And civilization requires the community to make decisions as to how principles are defined in terms of behavior. So it is with the church. We have traditionally referred to such definitions as "church standards." But its rules for the behavior of its members can never be exhaustive or intended to cover every contingency. Nor should all the rules be legislated. In other words, they are not all a test of fellowship. They may be designed to make a statement as to the church's stand with respect to Christian lifestyle and what it means to be a disciple of Christ.

While what has been said may suggest a reasonable approach to church standards, we are well aware that there have been and are churches and Christian groups that over-legislate the behavior of their members. This tends to freeze them in time and makes their statement with respect to principles irrelevant.

How the individual relates to the church in all this depends upon one's attitude toward the church. Does the body of Christ have a wisdom that we as individuals do not have? Has the Holy Spirit been promised to the church even as it has to us? Are we willing to concede that, though we might disagree, we love and need the fellowship of the body and therefore are willing to surrender our independence on a particular point of difference? Or are we so convicted that the truth we hold cannot be compromised? If so, there may be no other alternative but to leave the fellowship or be disfellowshiped by the church. There are times when this is as it should be. Without such conviction and consequences there would have been no Protestant Reformation.

On the other hand, there is the possibility that by remaining in the church and relating to the family in true Christian love we may bring about a reformation. This too has happened. The freedom of the individual to decide and make choices is a gift that God does not violate. It is integral to His plan of salvation. We are and will be judged on the basis of our decisions and choices.

How, then, shall we decide with respect to modesty? How shall we dress? It is no good to say, "How people see me is not my responsibility." It *is* our responsibility because our intention is not to attract attention to self but rather to Christ. We violate that principle when our appearance is either so drab and severe that it is ugly, or too glitzy and gaudy or sexually provocative.

With respect to stewardship, how shall we use the possessions God has provided? Here modesty is also relevant, as are honesty and faithfulness. What is Caesar's and what is the Lord's? Is staying out of debilitating debt a matter of stewardship? With respect to worldliness, how shall we relate to what the world offers in entertainment, pleasure, indulgence of appetite, and habit-forming gratifications that destroy body and soul?

When we are confronted with a question concerning whether or not our behavior is in keeping with Christian principle, to justify what we are doing or to seek to dismiss the question with an appeal to "grace through faith" versus "law" is a blatant cop-out. *Grace versus law is not the issue. How the principle is defined in terms of behavior is the issue.* Righteousness by faith is not license to disobey God. Let's stay with the issue and not jump to something irrelevant for our defense. Are we prepared to deny the imperative of growth in Christian behavior as it relates to *being saved* and degrade the gospel for the sake of defending some cherished pleasure? However, where there is room for difference of opinion as to what behavior correctly defines a principle, the loving Christian will not respond with judgment and damnation. Too often, at this point, we find it very easy to judge one another by our own standards. Patience, caring, and sharing is the better way. Resolution often takes time.

It is when we over-legislate rules that define principles in terms of behavior that the charge "legalism" becomes relevant and justified. Isn't it this that generates the greatest hostility?

Perfection

In the Sermon on the Mount, quoted above, Jesus said we must be perfect even as our heavenly Father is perfect (Matt. 5:48). How is that possible? Is that how we must live?

To begin with, we need to see the statement in its context. Jesus had been talking of loving our enemies and praying for those who persecute us so that we may be like the Father in heaven who makes His sun rise on the evil and on the good and sends rain on the just and unjust. It is widely believed that Jesus' statement about perfection had to do with this kind of love. We are to be perfect in love. What that means we shall see in the following chapter.

Be that as it may, we need to be aware that the Greek word in the New Testament translated "perfect" is *teleios,* which may mean "perfect," "complete," or "mature," depending upon the context. The KJV almost always translates *teleios* as "perfect." For instance, Colossians 1:28: ". . . that we may present every man *perfect* in Christ Jesus." Other versions do otherwise. While the NIV agrees with the KJV, the RSV reads, ". . . that we may present every man *mature* in Christ." And the NASB reads, ". . . that we may present every man *complete* in Christ." Where the KJV reads, "unto a *perfect* man," in Ephesians 4:13, the other versions use the word *mature.* According to the KJV, Philippians 3:12 reads as follows: "Not as though I had already attained, either were already *perfect. . . .*" But then in verse 15 it says, "Let us therefore, as many as be *perfect*, be thus minded. . . ." In writing this, why does Paul say in verse 12 that he is not yet perfect and yet in verse 15 identify with those who are perfect? Other versions escape the dilemma by translating *telios* differently in the two verses. The NIV and the RSV translate it "perfect" in verse 12 and "mature" in verse 15.

Is perfection possible? Would Jesus call for it if it weren't? Isn't it our desire to grow into the likeness of Christ? But when we try to measure "sinless perfection" in terms of a "complete" list of sins that must be overcome, including those that violate all the rules which define principles mentioned above, we tend to go beyond Scripture and become good Pharisees. Moreover, I have not seen two such lists that are in "perfect agreement," making the whole endeavor quite pointless.

Sinlessness in 1 John

Two most dramatic statements that have to do with sinlessness are found in 1 John 3:6, 9: "No one who abides in him sins; no one who sins has either seen him or known him." And, "No one born of God commits sin; for God's nature abides in him, and he cannot sin because he is born of God." This is freedom from sinning.

But wait, how can John say this when he writes in 1 John 2:1, "My little children, I am writing this to you so that you may not sin; but *if any one does sin*, we have an advocate with the Father, Jesus Christ the righteous . . ."? Or what does he mean when he writes, "If anyone sees his brother committing what is not a mortal sin, he will ask, and God will give him life for those whose sin is not mortal" (5:16)? In short, why does John claim a sinless perfection for the Christian believer in 3:6, 9 but not in 2:2 or 5:16?

John's teaching here seems to be contradictory, and through the years there have been numerous suggestions for solutions to the problem. I will not examine these in a scholarly review of the literature at this point but will offer an interpretation that comes from an awareness of that literature and an examination of the text, giving careful consideration to exegetical and contextual concerns.[8]

The most common interpretation among conservative students of the Bible is that the verb for "sin" in 1 John 3:6, 9 is in the present tense, which, according to the Greek language, indicates continuing action. Hence, the children of God do not "continue in sin." They are not *habitual* sinners. While this may be true to a point, using this analysis to support the thesis offers serious problems. The question remains, Is his use of the word "sin" in 1 John 2:1 the same as in 3:6, 9? It would seem that there is more to John's doctrine of sin than is brought to light by an analysis of verb tenses. Note the following:

Two Kinds of Children:

In Chapter 3, John writes with two distinct and radically different groups of people in mind. This is clear from the first verse: "See what love the Father has given us, that we should be called children of God [the first group]; and so we are. The reason why the world [the second group] does not know us is that it did not know him." In verse 10 it is clarified that the term "the world" as used here means "the children of the devil."

While in other portions of the epistle, John may make reference to some particular heresy or body of heretics, that is not the case in 1 John 3. Here he has in mind all people on the face of the earth who may be identified as either "children of God" or "the world" (children of the devil). The children of God are those whom he has previously referred to as "you" or "we" in 1 John 1, 2—those who, according to the Gospel of John, have become such through faith in Jesus Christ. ("But to all who received him, who believe in his name, he gave power to become children of God" [John 1:12].)

This way of dividing the human race is typical of Jesus. Consider again the two passages from John's Gospel where he quotes Jesus as saying, "If the world hates you, know that it has hated me before it hated you. If you were of the world, the world would love its own; but because you are not of the world, but I chose you out of the world, therefore the world hates you" (John 15:18, 19). And, "I have manifested thy name to the men whom thou gavest me out of the world. . . . I am praying for them; I am not praying for the world but for those whom thou hast given me, for they are thine. . . . I have given them thy word; and the world has hated them because they are not of the world, even as I am not of the world. I do not pray that thou shouldst take them out of the world, but that thou shouldst keep them from the evil one" (John 17:5-15).

John not only makes this distinction between world and children of God in 1 John 3, but between the world and God Himself in Chapter 2 (quoted previously): "Do not love the world or the things in the world. If any one loves the world, love for the Father is not in him. For all that is in the world, the lust of the flesh and the lust of the eyes and the pride of life, is not of the Father but is of the world" (vv. 15, 16).

The Meaning of "every one":

While John may identify two kinds of children, doesn't he say that "*every one* who commits sin is guilty of lawlessness" (3:4)? Yes, but "every one" in this context does not include the children of God. What we so easily fail to see is that "every one" in 3:3 and "every one" in 3:4 have different antecedents.

"Every one who thus hopes in him purifies himself as he is pure" (v. 3) refers to "God's children" (v. 1). "Every one who commits sin is guilty of lawlessness" (v. 4) refers to "the world" (v. 1).

To put it another way, the flow of the text will reveal that there is a parallel comparison between the two mutually exclusive groups. The first "every one" refers to one group (the children of God), while the other "every one" refers to the other group (the world—the children of the devil).

Two Kinds of Sinning:

As John identifies two kinds of children, so he defines sin (*hamartia*) in two different ways:

1. In 1 John 3:4 he says, "sin (*hamartia*) is lawlessness (*anomia*)." The term *anomia* is used in Romans 6:19 with reference to the human condition or disposition before baptism or the new birth: "For just as you once yielded your members to impurity (*anomia*) and to greater and greater impurity (*anomia*), so now yield your members to righteousness for sanctification." In 2 Corinthians 6:14 it is used with reference to "unbelievers": "Do not be mismated with unbelievers. For what partnership have righteousness and iniquity (*anomia*)?" Thus, every one who sins (*anomia*) is every one who is not a child of God.

Moreover, notice in Romans 7, notice how Paul characterizes sin and his relationship to the law before he was delivered from "this body of death" through Jesus Christ: "Did that which is good, then, bring death to me? By no means! It was sin, working death in me through what is good, in order that sin might be shown to be sin, and through the commandment might become *sinful beyond measure*" (vv. 12, 13).

2. In 1 John 5:17 John says, "all wrongdoing *(adikia =* unrighteousness) is sin *(hamartia)."* And this wrongdoing or unrighteousness is the sin from which the children of God are cleansed. "If we confess our sins, he is faithful and just, and will forgive our sins and cleanse us from all unrighteousness *(adikia)"* (1 John 1:9).

It is this unrighteousness, which John has defined as sin, that is spoken of in Chapter 1:8: "If we say we have no sin, we deceive ourselves, and the truth is not in us." In verse 10: "If we say we have not sinned, we make him a liar, and his word is not in us." And in Chapter 2:1: "My little children, I am writing this to you so that you may not sin; but if any one does sin. . . ."

Thus, everyone who is a child of God may sin *(adikia =* wrongdoing or unrighteousness), but does not sin *(anomia =* lawlessness). That is why John can say in Chapter 3:6, 9 that those who abide in Him (Jesus) and those who are born of God do not sin (having defined sin as *anomia* in verse 4).

The Sin That Is Mortal and the Sin That Is Not Mortal:

"If any one sees his brother committing what is not a mortal sin, he will ask, and God will give him life for those whose sin is not mortal. There is sin which is mortal; I do not say that one is to pray for that" (1 John 5:16). Attempts to explain what this means have run full spectrum, all the way from a cataloging of sins as to their degree of heinousness, to the unpardonable sin—the sin against the Holy Spirit (see Matt. 12:31). I would like to suggest, however, that there is an answer in the epistle itself.

In the passage quoted above (1 John 5:16), John looks back to the thought he expressed in Chapter 2:1, 2: "My little children, I am writing this to you so that you may not sin; but if any one does sin, we have an advocate with the Father, Jesus Christ the righteous; and he is the expiation for our sins, and not for ours only but also for the sins of the whole world." While Jesus made an "expiation" (atonement) for the whole world, He is an "advocate" (pleader) only for the "little children." Thus, it is because the children of God have an *advocate* that there is sin that is *not* mortal, and because the world does not have such an advocate there is sin that *is* mortal.

A double standard? Perhaps the strongest objection that may be raised to this interpretation of 1 John is that it seems to create a double standard—one for the children of God and another for the children of the devil. At least a part of the answer to that objection is found in the fact that according to the New Testament, being a Christian certainly does make a difference, and that difference is more than acts of obedience versus acts of disobedience. It involves a new orientation to life—a turning to God and an acceptance of His sovereignty, and a turning away from Satan and the world. It follows, then, that the behavior growing out of that orientation must be seen and judged accordingly.

This is not to say that the children of the devil cannot become children of God. Since Christ's atonement is for the whole world, anyone, anytime, anywhere can be saved from alienation from God as long as probation lasts. Furthermore, this approach does not diminish regard for the seriousness of sin in the life of the children of God. To speak of sin that is not mortal is not a negation of Paul's statement that "the wages of sin is death" (Rom. 6:23). The only way for a Christian's sin to be "not unto death" is for the sin to be forgiven through the priestly ministry of Christ. In instances when the child of God is struggling with a sin that is so easily besetting or clings so closely (Heb. 12:1) or has sinned unwittingly, ignorantly, or unintentionally, John encourages intercessory prayer (1 John 5:16). But willful, unrepented sin is not overlooked and excused. For such sin there is no advocate. "For if we sin deliberately after receiving the knowledge of the truth, there no longer remains a sacrifice for sins, but a fearful prospect of judgment . . ." (Heb. 10:26).

There is a sense in which the interpretation given here does support the argument that the child of God does not *continue* in sin. But it does so through an analysis of context and meaning of language or word usage rather than an appeal to the verb tense alone, which has its difficulties.

The children of God ought to be the happiest people in the world. Because they are God's children, God hangs in there with them; in a very special sense He is on their side. They may at times be guilty of unrighteousness. They may make mistakes in moments of weakness when tempted by the evil one, but as children of God they are not guilty of lawlessness.

What we have been considering is complicated by the fact that we live in a society which, to a large degree, determines right from wrong by whether or not it feels good. "If it feels good, how can it be wrong?" or as someone has characterized our contemporary moral code, "If it feels good, do it. And if you get in trouble, blame it on someone else." Turn on the television or radio or go to the movies, and let the media do your thinking for you. You can't be pious or spiritual if you are too rational. Being created in the image of God with a high degree of intelligence, the power to think and to do, is of no real value. It is too difficult, takes too much effort.

Well, pardon me. If you have reached this point in reading this book, you know I don't buy it. We've been given heads as well as hearts. Thinking things through is a privilege and a responsibility. The Holy Spirit moves upon both our minds and our hearts. Satan would like nothing better than to have a falsehood propagated as a pious truth. Such deception is one of his specialties, and our only defense is continued careful and prayerful study under the *guidance* of the Holy Spirit.

The law cannot save us. It never could. But there would be no need for grace without it. We do not have grace without law. Neither do we have faith without law. "Do we then overthrow the law by this faith? By no means! On the contrary, we uphold the law" (Rom. 3:31).

Where in all of this is the good news? Knowing how to live as a Christian, making the decisions we have to make from day to day can be burdensome and even depressing because of Satan's determination to deceive us. But here again, Christ is the answer. "Jesus then said to the Jews who had believed in him, 'If you continue in my word, you are truly my disciples, and you will know the truth, and the truth will make you free.'. . . So if the Son makes you free, you will be free indeed" (John 8:31, 36). That's the good news, and there is more to come.

7

Living the Christian Way

"For in Christ Jesus neither circumcision nor uncircumcision is of any avail, but faith working through love *(agape)*" (Gal. 5:6). To young Timothy, Paul writes, "Follow the pattern of the sound words which you have heard from me, in the faith and love which are in Christ Jesus; guard the truth that has been entrusted to you by the Holy Spirit who dwells within us" (2 Tim. 1:13, 14). In Christ there is faith and love, and faith is made effective or energized *(energoumene,* from *energeo* or *energeia)* through love. What a revelation! May we conclude, therefore, that while we are saved by grace through faith, that faith is ineffective without love? Believing is not enough; the devils also believe and tremble (James 2:19). But why does love make faith effective or why does love energize faith? Because it is "in Christ."

A woman was giving testimony in a meeting, and in her testimony said, "I don't have a religion, I have a relationship." In response, the room resounded with *amen*s. I joined them. Whatever she may have meant by "religion," I thought it was a wonderful testimony because one who is being saved does not only believe in a set of doctrines but has a profound relationship—"in Christ." And it is in that relationship that faith is made effective through love.

That makes "love" of critical importance, doesn't it? Just what is Christian love?

In Christian love *(agape)* there are at least two indispensable characteristics: *affection* and *commitment.* "You shall love the Lord your God with all your heart, and with all your soul, and with all your mind" (Matt. 22:37).

"With all your heart" has to do with our feelings, our affective nature.

"With all your soul" has to do with our whole being.

"With all your mind" has to do with our intellect, our cognitive nature.

We know very well the affective. The world we live in is obsessed with romantic love. A man and a woman are drawn together by great amorous feeling for each other. Movies, books, and sitcoms on television are driven by it, live by it. This must impress us with how it can be cheapened and depraved through commercialization, but must not diminish our appreciation for the deep feeling and affection we may have in love—for God, for family, and for one another.

But what has happened to the cognitive with which we make commitment? Why is the divorce rate so high? All too often it is because of a lack of commitment on the part of one or both spouses. Why do people want to live together without taking the wedding vows in public? Again, all too often it is because they don't want to make the commitment. When the feeling fades they want to walk away from the relationship without cost or great inconvenience.

How different is God's love for us. It is loaded with affection *and* commitment. For God so loved the world—*affection*—that He gave His only Son—*commitment!* Of Jesus, who came to reveal God's character, we read in reference to the raising of Lazarus in John 11:33-36, "When Jesus saw her weeping, and the Jews who came with her also weeping, he was deeply moved in spirit and troubled; and he said, 'Where have you laid him?' They said to him, 'Lord, come and see.' Jesus wept. So the Jews said, *'See how he loved him!'*"—*affection!* Also, we read in John 13:1, "Now before the feast of the

Passover, when Jesus knew that his hour had come to depart out of this world to the Father, having loved his own who were in the world, *he loved them to the end"—commitment!*

There is a word that epitomizes this kind of relationship. It is the word "discipleship." In discipleship, radical commitment defines the love relationship.

The Slavery That Is Freedom

Paul speaks of his radical commitment to Christ in terms of slavery. In Romans 1:1 he introduces himself as "a servant *(doulos* = slave) of Jesus Christ." So also do James (James 1:1), Peter (2 Peter 1:1), and Jude (Jude 1:1).

"Slavery." That doesn't sound like freedom, does it? Yet it does when we realize that slavery in Christ is the only freedom we will ever know. There are two reasons why this is so:

1. "In Christ" we are free from bondage to our sinful nature. When we are born again we are free to choose to obey Him and are empowered to do so.

2. Unless we are "in Christ" we are slaves to sin. Satan never hesitates to bring us under his influence and use us whether we consent or not. It does not suit his purpose to honor our freedom of choice.

It is sad that the "world" does not realize this. There is no such privilege as neutrality in the great conflict between Christ and Satan. Jesus said to those who rejected Him, "You are of your father the devil, and your will is to do your father's desires" (John 8:44). He also said, "Truly, truly, I say to you, every one who commits sin is a slave to sin. The slave does not continue in the house for ever; the son continues for ever. So if the Son makes you free, you will be free indeed" (John 8:34-36). To be a slave of Christ is to be set free in Him. It is to be set free from alienation from God. It is to be set free from a life of disobedience.

Paul writes in Galatians 5:1, "For freedom Christ has set us free; stand fast therefore, and do not submit again to a yoke of slavery. . . ." This is said with reference to meaningless ceremony and tradition, but in verse 13 it says, "For you were called to freedom, brethren, only do not use your freedom as an opportunity for the flesh, but through love *(agape)* be servants *(douleuete = slaves)* of one another." For freedom Christ has set us free to love—to love in a radical, Christian way.

To love this way is to be free from fear: "So we know and believe the love God has for us. God is love, and he who abides in love abides in God, and God abides in him. In this is love perfected with us, that we may have confidence for the day of judgment, because as he is so are we in the world. *There is no fear in love, but perfect love casts out fear"* (1 John 4:16-18).

A rich young ruler comes to Jesus with a question: "Good Teacher, what shall I do to inherit eternal life?"

To which Jesus replies, "You know the commandments: 'Do not commit adultery, Do not kill, Do not steal, Do not bear false witness, Honor your father and mother.'"

"All these I have observed from my youth," says the ruler.

"Wonderful!" is Jesus' response. "I can't ask for more. You are a model young man, ready for heaven." Not quite. What Jesus really says is rather shocking: "One thing you still lack. Sell all that you have and distribute to the poor, and you will have treasure in heaven; and come, follow me" (Luke 18:18, 20-22).

Sounds rather radical, doesn't it? Do we really have to sell all that we have and give to the poor in order to have eternal life? The answer is found in the words "follow me." What the rich young ruler lacked was a saving *commitment!* He was a rule keeper, a "check-lister"; he was committed to keeping commandments but not to Jesus Christ. Keeping the rules was good. Jesus didn't rebuke him for that. What he lacked was a Christian love relationship. He was not a disciple.

Obedience is faith energized by love. Works is belief energized by fear. When Jesus comes and says, "Follow me," do it! It is the wisest choice you will ever make.

Lest we hesitate to think of Jesus as a radical when it comes to discipleship, listen to what He has to say in Luke 14:26, 27, 33: "If any one comes to me and does not hate his own father and mother and wife and children and brothers and sisters, yes, and even his own life, he cannot be my disciple. Whoever does not bear his own cross and come after me, cannot be my disciple. . . . So therefore, whoever of you does not renounce all that he has cannot be my disciple." Sound too severe, does it? Again, the answer is found in the last sentence, which states that whoever does not renounce all that he has cannot be Jesus' disciple. Whether or not we are separated from family and bear a cross unto death is not really the point. Are we ready to do so if that's what it takes? That's the point. That is commitment.

If the relationship of obedience to salvation is not yet clear, note what Jesus says in Luke 6:46: "Why do you call me 'Lord, Lord,' and not do what I tell you?" What Jesus tells us does not make us His disciple. It is *doing* what He tells us. "Not every one who says to me, 'Lord, Lord,' shall enter the kingdom of heaven, but he who does the will of my Father who is in heaven" (Matt. 7:21). Not everyone who knows the will of the Father will enter the kingdom of heaven, but he who *does* the will of the Father. The law of God tells us what God would have us do, but that does not save us. It is doing what God would have us do *in Christ* that gives us entrance to the kingdom of heaven.

It is after the resurrection. Jesus is standing on the beach of the Sea of Tiberias. The disciples have been fishing all night and have caught nothing. As they near the shore Jesus says to them, "Children, have you any fish?" They say, "No." So He says to them, "Cast the net on the right side of the boat, and you will find some." They do as he says, and the fish fill the net so that they cannot haul it in. Then John says to Peter, "It is the Lord!" and Peter goes into shock. He must have, because he does something that otherwise he would not do. It doesn't make sense. He *puts on* his clothes and *jumps into the water!* But he soon recovers, and when Jesus asks for some of the fish, Peter goes and gets them.

Now Jesus is not playing games. What He does comes from His heart of love. He knows the disciples are tired and discouraged. It is no fun to fish all night and catch nothing, especially for professional fishermen. So He builds a fire, cooks some fish, warms some bread, and invites them to have breakfast. There is no question. This is Jesus and they know it. They have been with Him as His disciples, and they know that He loves them. But they are to learn again what His kind of love is all about.

When they finish breakfast, Jesus says to Simon Peter, "Simon, son of John, do you love *(agape)* me more than these?" To which Peter responds, "Yes, Lord; you know that I love *(phileo)* you." And Jesus says, "Feed my lambs."

Note the difference in the word for love here. Jesus uses the word *agape;* Peter answers with the word *phileo.* Perhaps this is coincidental—a scribal glitch or the whim of the textual copier. But maybe not. Could it be that Peter did not feel qualified to use "agape"? After all, he had denied his Lord after claiming he would defend Him to the death. Be that as it may, there is something to be noted here that is relevant to our understanding of discipleship.

Jesus asks the question two more times. "Do you love me? Tend my sheep." "Do you love *(phileo)* me? Feed my sheep." (The third time He asks the question, Jesus uses the word for love that Peter has been using.) (For the above story, see John 21:1-19.)

God's love is kind and long-suffering, isn't it? He knows our weaknesses and our frustrations, but He doesn't turn away in disgust. He keeps in touch; He doesn't let us go. Here is a love relationship. "Do you love me?"—affection. "Feed my sheep"—commitment. At the end of this encounter with His disciples Jesus says, "Follow me."

But we're not through with Peter yet. Right after the above in verses 20-22 it says, "Peter turned and saw following them the disciple whom Jesus loved, who had lain close to his breast at the supper. . . . When Peter saw him, he said to Jesus, 'Lord, what about this man?' Jesus said to him, 'If it is my will that he remain until I come, what is that to you? Follow me!'" "What is that to you?" How often we become distracted by questions and concerns that are irrelevant. We need to keep our focus on what really matters. A life "in Christ" is a life of discipleship, of following Jesus, growing up *in Him*—with deep affection and commitment. Can we do it? Yes, but only because of *His* affection and commitment to us.

We are well acquainted with Christ's promise to come again and receive us unto Himself (John 14:1-3), but notice what He says later in verses 19-21: "I will not leave you desolate; I will come to you. Yet a little while, and the world will see me no more, but you will see me; because I live, you will live also. In that day you will know that I am in my Father, and you in me and I in you. He who has my commandments and keeps them, he it is who loves me; and he who loves me will be loved by my Father, and I will love him and manifest myself to him." And these words from John 16:33: "I have said this to you, that in me you may have peace. In the world you have tribulation; but be of good cheer, I have overcome the world."

Have you read the intercessory, high priestly prayer, of Jesus for his disciples lately? We ought to read it every now and then. It is a wonderful source of encouragement because it shows *His* affection and commitment of which we speak. "I am praying for them; I am not praying for the world but for those whom thou hast given me, for they are thine; all mine are thine, and thine are mine, and I am glorified in them. And now I am no more in the world, but they are in the world, and I am coming to thee. Holy Father, keep them in thy name, which thou hast given me, that they may be one, even as we are one. . . . I do not pray that thou shouldst take them out of the world, but that thou shouldst keep them from the evil one. They are not of the world, even as I am not of the world. Sanctify them in the truth; thy word is truth. . . . O righteous Father, the world has not known thee, but I have known thee; and these know that thou hast sent me. I made known to them thy name, and I will make it known, *that the love with which thou hast loved me may be in them, and I in them"* (John 17:9-11, 15-17, 25, 26). It is that love that makes faith effective.

Keeping Together What Belongs Together

Up to this point, for the most part, I have treated reconciliation and transformation separately. We come to Christ for reconciliation, we are justified, and then we live in Christ to grow up and be transformed into His likeness. Traditionally, we have taught this using a slightly different terminology—justification and sanctification. Unfortunately, we have too consistently considered them mutually exclusive. That is to say, once we are justified we are saved, and we go on from there with no need for justification again as we strive for perfection (unless, of course, we backslide and "fall from grace").

This, I believe, is a misunderstanding. While our salvation begins with justification (when we are reconciled to God by faith) followed by transformation, the two coexist throughout the salvation experience. Consider the following:

We have been reconciled and justified. We are children of God. Through the power Christ makes available, we "walk as children of light" (Eph. 5:8)—we obey God, we keep His commandments. Now notice how justification continues to affirm our reconciliation: "If we say we have fellowship with him while we walk in darkness, we lie and do not live according to the truth; but if we walk in the light, as he is in the light, we have fellowship with one another, and *the blood of Jesus his Son cleanses us from all sin*" (1 John 1:6, 7).

As we walk in the light we make mistakes; we fail to do the will of God at times because we are growing—we're not there yet. And because we make mistakes, because we sin, we are guilty of unrighteousness. That being true, what do we need? We need to be cleansed from that unrighteousness. How? "If we confess our sins, he is faithful and just, and will forgive our sins and *cleanse us from all unrighteousness*" (1 John 1:9). He makes us right again. Cleansing us from all unrighteousness, cleansing us from all sin, is what justification is all about. Our reconciliation is affirmed as we walk in the light—as we are being saved. When we come to Christ we are saved because of the atonement, justification, and sanctification He provides through His death on the cross, and every time we fall or fail to obey, these provisions make forgiveness possible. "He is the source of your life in Christ Jesus, whom God made our wisdom, our righteousness and sanctification and redemption" (1 Cor. 1:30).

Faith and grace and works are not irreconcilable. We need to think of salvation in holistic terms. It is my conviction that this is how we will come to a desperately needed consensus on this most vital truth. Analysis has its place as we seek understanding, but without synthesis we never get up and walk. We can take a clock apart to see how it works, but it will not work until we put it back together again. The whole is always more than the sum of its parts. Notice how Colossians 1:21-23 brings the parts together: "And you, who once were estranged and hostile in mind, *doing evil deeds, he has now reconciled* in his body of flesh by his death, in order to present you *holy and blameless and irreproachable before him, provided that you continue in the faith,* stable and steadfast, not shifting from the hope of the gospel which you heard, which was preached to every creature under heaven, and of which I, Paul, became a minister." And to this we must add Colossians 2:6: "As therefore you have received Christ Jesus the Lord, so live in him, rooted and built up in him and established in the faith, just as you were taught, abounding in thanksgiving."

One Day at a Time

Personally, I have been encouraged by something Jesus said in Matthew 6:34: "Therefore do not be anxious about tomorrow, for tomorrow will be anxious for itself. Let the day's own trouble be sufficient for the day."

This counsel, according to the context, has to do with our physical or material needs, but I have found assurance by applying it to my spiritual needs as well. Don't be anxious about tomorrow, for tomorrow will have enough anxiety of its own. In other words, live in Christ *one day at a time.* There is no need for us to worry ourselves into a chronic state of anxiety about how sin-free we must be before probation closes prior to the coming of Christ. If we abide in Christ day by day, one day at a time, we will be whatever we should be—at the time of the close of probation or at the time of death, which are both, in reality, the same as far as our destiny is concerned.

Spelled out in practical terms, here is what I have found helpful in applying the relevant counsel given by God:

1. Begin the day "in Christ" and "set your mind on the things of the Spirit."

"But thanks be to God, who *in Christ* always leads us in triumph, and through us spreads the fragrance of the knowledge of him everywhere" (2 Cor. 2:14). "Therefore, if any one is *in Christ*, he is a new creation; the old has passed away, behold, the new has come" (2 Cor. 5:17).

"For those who live according to the flesh set their minds on the things of the flesh, but those who *live according to the Spirit set their minds on the things of the Spirit.* To set the mind on the flesh is death, but to set the mind on the Spirit is life and peace. . . .

"But you are not in the flesh, you are in the Spirit, if in fact the Spirit of God dwells in you. Any one who does not have the Spirit of Christ does not belong to him. But if Christ is in you, although your bodies are dead because of sin, your spirits are alive because of righteousness" (Rom. 8:5, 6, 9, 10). Those who live according to the Spirit set their minds on the things of the Spirit for the guidance that Jesus promised through the Spirit. "But the Counselor, the Holy Spirit, whom the Father will send in my name, He will teach you all things, and bring to your remembrance all that I have said to you. Peace I leave with you; my peace I give to you; not as the world gives do I give to you. Let not your hearts be troubled, neither let them be afraid" (John 14:26, 27).

Paul, in Colossians 3:1-4 again counsels us, "If then you have been raised with Christ, *seek the things that are above*, where Christ is, seated at the right hand of God. *Set your minds on things that are above*, not on things that are on earth. For you have died, and *your life is hid with Christ in God*. When Christ who is our life appears, then you also will appear with him in glory."

2. Throughout the day, grow in the knowledge of God's will and learn how to cooperate with Him when dealing with temptation.

"And so, from the day we heard of it, we have not ceased to pray for you, asking that you may be *filled with the knowledge of his will* in all spiritual wisdom and understanding, to lead a life worthy of the Lord, fully pleasing him, bearing fruit in every good work and *increasing in the knowledge of God*" (Col. 1:9, 10).

It has always been helpful for me to learn by example, and, fortunately, the one who wrote the above tells us of his experience and gives his counsel. I quote again rather extensively from Paul's epistle to the Philippians:

"But whatever gain I had, I counted as loss for the sake of Christ. Indeed I count everything as loss because of the surpassing worth of knowing Christ Jesus my Lord. For his sake I have suffered the loss of all things, and count them as refuse, in order that I may gain Christ *and be found* in him, not having a righteousness of my own, based on law, but that which is through faith in Christ, the righteousness from God that depends on faith; that I may know him and the power of his resurrection, and may share his sufferings, becoming like him in his death, that if possible I may attain the resurrection from the dead.

"Not that I have already obtained this or am already

perfect; but I press on to make it my own, because Christ Jesus has made me his own. Brethren, *I do not consider that I have made it my own;* but one thing I do, forgetting what lies behind and straining forward to what lies ahead, *I press on toward the goal* for the prize of the upward call of God in Christ Jesus" (Phil. 3:7-14).

Downcast because of adversity and frustration? No way! Note his call to assurance and hope in Philippians 4:4-12: "Rejoice in the Lord always; again I will say, Rejoice. Let all men know your forbearance. The Lord is at hand. Have no anxiety about anything, but in everything by prayer and supplication with thanksgiving let your requests be made known to God. And the *peace of God,* which passes all under-standing, will *keep your hearts and your minds in Christ Jesus.*

"Finally, brethren, whatever is true, whatever is honor-able, whatever is just, whatever is pure, whatever is lovely, whatever is gracious, if there is any excellence, if there is anything worthy of praise, think about these things. What you have learned and received and heard and seen in me, do; and the God of peace will be with you.

"I rejoice in the Lord greatly that now at length you have revived your concern for me; you were indeed concerned for me, but you had no opportunity. Not that I complain of want; for I have learned, in whatever state I am, to be content. I know how to be abased, and I know how to abound; in any and all circumstances I have learned the secret of facing plenty and hunger, abundance and want." And now comes that one-liner that I have used and commented on before—one of the most encouraging declarations in all of Scripture, "I can do all things in him who strengthens *(endynamites)* me" (v. 13). That is why Paul can urge upon us a life of holi-ness. Christian values are not negotiable.

Concerning temptation, Paul offers this counsel:

First, "Put on the Lord Jesus Christ, and make no provision for the flesh, to gratify its desires" (Rom. 13:14). Every day we are confronted with temptation. Satan never sleeps and never tires of engaging the Christian in combat. When confronted, we should remember, "No temptation has overtaken you that is not common to man. God is faithful, and he will not let you be tempted beyond your strength, but with the temptation will also provide the way of escape, that you may be able to endure it" (1 Cor. 10:13). We must learn to make Christ our refuge as a habit. "Put on the Lord Jesus Christ," is the first thing Romans 14:13 admonishes us to do.

Second, ". . . make no provision for the flesh, to gratify its desires." We cannot win by playing with temptation, taking comfort in the fact that temptation itself is not sin, but yielding to temptation is sin. When possible, we should take measures to avoid temptation and keep Satan from taking advantage.

For instance, Joe has decided that going to a heavy metal rock concert offers too many opportunities for gratifying the desires of the flesh—that which is carnal and not spiritual. It is not something which he would invite Jesus to do with him. But on his walk to work each day, he passes in front of the music hall where such concerts are performed regularly, and out front, on billboards as big as life, the stars, musicians, and their performances are advertised with every enticement Madison Avenue can offer. He stops for a moment to read and look at the advertising, determined that he will not attend but simply enjoy the temptation. One evening on his way home he passes the music hall and discovers that a performance is about to begin. He stops again to enjoy the temptation and before he knows it he is edging closer to the window where tickets are being sold. "After all, one concert isn't going to kill me. I don't go regularly. Just this once won't hurt." Well, what comes next? You know, don't you?

How could this have been avoided? What could he have done? First of all, he could have walked by the music hall without reading the "come-ons." Perhaps it would have helped to walk on the other side of the street. Or maybe the best thing would have been to walk a different route to work. If he has "put on Christ," the Holy Spirit is probably suggesting something like this. But the decision is his to make. It isn't going to happen automatically. God is not going to do for him what he can do "in Christ." In cooperating with Christ, he will make a heavy investment of physical and mental effort. This is part of his total commitment.

How is it with us? We may feel embarrassed going another route because it is an admission of weakness. We like to think of ourselves as being stronger than that. Think again! That is precisely what Satan wants us to think. Never forget, we are no match for him; he has been at it too long and he knows our weaknesses. We may have to take time off to sleep, but he doesn't. In the power available in Christ, *decide* and *do*. Make *no provision* for the flesh to gratify its desires.

3. At the end of the day, accept God's forgiveness.

Forgiveness is not an easy thing to accept. Pride makes it difficult because it confirms our weakness and failure. Shame also makes it difficult because we feel so unworthy that we can't believe that someone cares enough about us or loves us enough to really forgive us. This is especially true when we have confessed to the same wrong again and again.

But God does care that much. We cannot take advantage of God; we cannot con Him. God is not permissive. But God *never* refuses to forgive one who comes to Him in real sorrow and contrition, *never*—seventy times seventy times seventy times seventy!

This being true, before we go to sleep at night we may

confess our sins, ask forgiveness for any mistakes we may have made during the day, and know that should life come to an end during the night, before we awake to the new day, our salvation is secure in Christ.

It is our privilege to live a life of security in Christ. Begin the day with Him—set the mind on the things of the Spirit. Live each day in Him—grow in the knowledge of God, learn how to deal with temptation. End the day with Him—never doubt God's love and His willingness to forgive.

Are we in need of greater assurance? I know of no more encouraging and assuring passage of Scripture than the last eleven verses of Romans 8:

"We know that in everything God works for good with those who love him, who are called according to his purpose. For those whom he foreknew he also predestined to be conformed to the image of his Son, in order that he might be the first-born among many brethren. And those whom he predestined he also called; and those whom he called he also justified; and those whom he justified he also glorified.

"What then shall we say to this? If God is for us, who is against us? He who did not spare his own Son but gave him up for us all, will he not also give us all things with him? Who shall bring any charge against God's elect? It is God who justifies; who is to condemn? Is it Christ Jesus, who died, yes, who was raised from the dead, who is at the right hand of God, who indeed intercedes for us? Who shall separate us from the love of Christ? Shall tribulation, or distress, or persecution, or famine, or nakedness, or peril, or sword? As it is written,

'For thy sake we are being killed all the day long;
we are regarded as sheep to be slaughtered.'

"No, in all these things we are more than conquerors through him who loved us. For I am sure that neither death, nor life, nor angels, nor principalities, nor things present, nor things to come, nor powers, nor height, nor depth, nor anything else in all creation, will be able to separate us from the love of God in Christ Jesus our Lord" (vv. 28-39).

Growing up to salvation—transformation *is* righteousness by faith.

Glorification

8

Glorification

Mary is in prison. She had refused to renounce her faith in Jesus. It is a time of religious persecution.

Suddenly she feels the earth shake. Then the door to her cell comes open. She walks out into the prison yard and becomes conscious of a brightness in the sky. She looks up and sees a small cloud the size of a man's hand. The cloud grows larger as it comes closer to earth, and then she hears the sound of a trumpet, and suddenly she begins to rise from the earth. As she goes up she can see a cemetery not far away and notices with astonishment that graves have been opened. Then she sees Him, sitting on a throne surrounded by angels and descending on a cloud of angels. Now she knows what it is all about! With unspeakable joy she joins the host that has been raised from the dead and that has been translated as she has been.

An episode from Star Wars or a space odyssey? No way. This story depicts the fulfillment of a promise cherished by every believer and follower of Jesus: "Let not your heart be troubled: ye believe in God, believe also in me. In my Father's house are many mansions: if it were not so, I would have told you. I go to prepare a place for you. And if I go and prepare a place for you, I will come again, and receive you unto myself; that where I am, there ye may be also" (John 14:1-3, KJV).

This promise of Christ's return was to be given again when it was sorely needed. Jesus and His disciples had gathered together on the mount called Olivet. For some reason, the disciples were still not clear as to the future of Israel. And while Jesus was answering their question, ". . . as they were looking on, he was lifted up, and a cloud took him out of their sight" (Acts 1:9).

Well! What do you suppose followed? What would you have done? Just what the disciples did, because it was the natural thing to do. They stood there, gazing up into the heavens, when suddenly ". . . two men stood by them in white robes, and said, 'Men of Galilee, why do you stand looking into heaven? This Jesus, who was taken up from you into heaven, will come in the same way as you saw him go into heaven" (vv. 10, 11).

In his letter to Titus, Paul speaks of this as the "blessed hope." "For the grace of God has appeared for the salvation of all men, training us to renounce irreligion and worldly passions, and to live sober, upright, and godly lives in this world, *awaiting our blessed hope, the appearing of the glory of our great God and Savior Jesus Christ,* who gave himself for us to redeem us from iniquity and to purify for himself a people of his own who are zealous for good deeds" (Titus 2:11-14).

Moreover, in writing to those who "first believed," to the community of faith, to those therefore who "have been saved" and are "being saved," he writes of a salvation yet to come: "Besides this you know what hour it is, how it is full time now for you to wake from sleep. For *salvation is nearer to us now than when we first believed;* the night is far gone, the day is at hand" (Rom. 13:11, 12).

That salvation that is yet to come is confirmed in 1 Peter 1:3-5: "Blessed be the God and Father of our Lord Jesus Christ! By his great mercy we have been born anew to a living hope through the resurrection of Jesus Christ from the dead, and to an inheritance which is imperishable, undefiled, and unfading, kept in heaven for you, who by God's power are guarded through faith for a *salvation ready to be revealed in the last time.*" Also, in Hebrews 9:27, 28: "And just as it is appointed for men to die once, and after that the judgment, so Christ, having been offered once to bear the sins of many, will appear a second time, not to deal with sin but to *save* those who are eagerly waiting for him."

A Time of Judgment

When evil and immorality run rampant and innocent people suffer deprivation and destruction, the moral question is raised in anger and anguish, "How long, oh Lord, how long? Doesn't anybody care?" The answer is, "Yes! God does!"

Because He created a universe inhabited with intelligent beings, and because He created humankind in His image with the freedom to make moral choices (therefore making them accountable for those choices and their consequences), justice calls for judgment. Love requires it.

That is why Paul said, speaking in the middle of the Areopagus in Athens, "The times of ignorance God overlooked, but now he commands all men everywhere to repent, because he has fixed a day on which he will judge the world in righteousness by a man whom he has appointed, and of this he has given assurance to all men by raising him from the dead" (Acts 17:30, 31). And to the believers in Rome: "Why do you pass judgment on your brother? Or you, why do you despise your brother? For we shall all stand before the judgment seat of God; for it is written, 'As I live, says the Lord, every knee shall bow to me, and every tongue shall give praise to God.' So each of *us* shall give an account of himself to God" (Rom. 14:10-12).

But we should not be threatened by the judgment that is

to come. Jesus' prediction of a judgment that will take place at the time of His return is a word of hope to those who truly follow Him: "When the Son of man comes in his glory, and all the angels with him, then he will sit on his glorious throne. Before him will be gathered all the nations, and he will separate them one from another as a shepherd separates the sheep from the goats, and he will place the sheep at his right hand, but the goats at the left. Then the King will say to those at his right hand, 'Come, O blessed of my Father, inherit the kingdom prepared for you from the foundation of the world'" (Matt. 25:31-34).

An important portrayal of judgment found in Revelation 20:11, 12 offers great assurance: "Then I saw a great white throne and him who sat upon it; from his presence earth and sky fled away, and no place was found for them. And I saw the dead, great and small, standing before the throne, and books were opened. Also another book was opened, which is the book of life. And the dead were judged by what was written in the books, by what they had done." Note, a "book of life" is used in the judgment. This brings to mind an interesting passage from Malachi 3:16-18: "Then those who feared the Lord spoke with one another; the Lord heeded and heard them, and a book of remembrance was written before him of those who feared the Lord and thought on his name. 'They shall be mine, says the Lord of hosts, my special possession on the day when I act, and I will spare them as a man spares his son who serves him. Then once more you shall distinguish between the righteous and the wicked, between one who serves God and one who does not serve him.'"

What we learn from these texts is this: Before the *execution* of judgment, in a *pre-advent* judgment, the fate of those to be judged is written in books of record. One of the books is a "book of life" or a "book of remembrance" which contains the names of those who are "mine" (God's children). Of these God says, "I will spare them as a man spares his son who serves him." Moreover, it is because of this pre-advent judgment that the Son of man, when He comes and sits on His glorious throne, can separate the sheep from the goats and say, as in Revelation 22:12, "Behold, I am coming soon, bringing my recompense, to repay every one for what he has done."

Because the names of God's children are written in the "book of life," John can write in 1 John 2:28, "And now, little children, abide in him, so that *when he appears we may have confidence and not shrink from him in shame at his coming.*" And in Chapter 4:16-18: "So we know and believe the love God has for us. God is love, and he who abides in love abides in God, and God abides in him. In this is love perfected with us, *that we may have confidence for the day of judgment,* because as he is so are we in this world. There is no fear in love, but perfect love casts out fear." Note the words, "He who abides in love abides in God, and God abides in him." This gives us confidence because it brings to mind the words of Jesus quoted previously: "He who abides in me, and I in him, he it is that bears much fruit, for apart from me you can do nothing. . . . As the Father has loved me, so have I loved you; abide in my love. If you keep my commandments, you will abide in my love, just as I have kept my Father's commandments and abide in his love" (John 15:4, 5, 9, 10).

However sobering the coming of a day of judgment, we rejoice that the reign of sin in this world will soon be brought to an end. In His love and mercy, God will no longer tolerate the unspeakable suffering caused by selfishness, pride, and greed—the consequence of God-independence. In view of the judgment, the premier of choices is the decision to abide in Christ.

Glorification in the Day of Judgment

"I consider that the sufferings of this present time are not worth comparing with the glory that is to be revealed to us. For the creation waits with eager longing for the revealing of the sons of God; for the creation was subjected to futility, not of its own will but by the will of him who subjected it in hope; because the creation itself will be set free from its bondage to decay and obtain the glorious liberty of the children of God. We know that the whole creation has been groaning in travail together until now; and not only the creation, but we ourselves, who have the first fruits of the Spirit, groan inwardly as we *wait for adoption as sons, the redemption of our bodies*. For *in hope we are saved*" (Rom. 8:18-24).

"In hope we are saved." That applies to the whole plan of salvation, but never more than it does to our "adoption as sons, the redemption of our bodies." The second coming of Jesus is more than a time of judgment; it is the culmination of our hope in the face of death. It is the time when "the creation itself will be set free from its bondage to decay and obtain the *glorious* liberty of the children of God." It is a time of re-creation through resurrection and translation.

"But we would not have you ignorant, brethren, concerning those who are asleep, that you may not grieve as others do who have no hope. For since we believe that Jesus died and rose again, even so, through Jesus, God will bring with him those who have fallen asleep. For this we declare to you by the word of the Lord, that we who are alive, who are left until the coming of the Lord, shall not precede those who have fallen asleep. For the Lord himself will descend from heaven with a cry of command, with the archangel's call, and with the sound of the trumpet of God. And the dead in Christ will rise first; then we who are alive, who are left, shall be caught up together with them in the clouds to meet the Lord in the air; and so shall we always be with the Lord. *Therefore comfort one another with these words"* (1 Thess. 4:13-18). A resurrection, a translation, a reunion with loved ones who have been taken from us in death. What a promise! What a comfort! What a hope! Notice the words, "and so we shall always be with the Lord." Isn't that the cherished dream of every Christian, to be with the Jesus who loves us so? Notice it says "always"—to be with Him *always*.

"Lo! I tell you a mystery. We shall not all sleep, but we shall all be changed, in a moment, in the twinkling of an eye, at the last trumpet. For the trumpet will sound, and the dead will be raised imperishable, and we shall be changed. For this perishable nature must put on the imperishable, and this mortal nature must put on *immortality*. When the perishable puts on the imperishable, and the mortal puts on *immortality*, then shall come to pass the saying that is written: 'Death is swallowed up in victory.' 'O death, where is thy victory? O death, where is thy sting?'" (1 Cor. 15:51-55).

When the perishable puts on the imperishable and the mortal puts on immortality, death is swallowed up in victory. This is the third facet or "face" in God's plan for a full salvation. We "have been saved" through reconciliation. We are "being saved" through transformation. And in the salvation that is nearer now than when we first believed we "shall be saved" through the glory that is to be revealed—resurrection and translation. *"The last enemy to be destroyed is death"* (1 Cor. 15:26).

The Gift of Immortality

The Bible does not teach that humankind has inherent immortality and that an immortal soul, apart from the body, goes to glory at death, then returns at the second coming of

Christ to inhabit an immortalized body. Such a doctrine creates a ridiculous absurdity because it teaches that souls who have gone to heaven at death without a body are "with the Lord" in an incomplete and imperfect state from the time of death until the resurrection. Isn't one imperfect lifetime on earth enough without having to spend age upon age in heaven waiting for a body? Put in the simplest of terms, if the righteous dead already have immortality, why should it be given to them at the Second Coming? If they are "with the Lord" without the body, why do they need a body?

Is a mother who has died and gone to heaven conscious of what is happening on earth? Is she "looking down upon us"? If so, is her joy complete as she observes the lifestyle of her unsaved and ungodly son? Please, spare us that!

The doctrine of the inherent immortality of the soul is bound to have its effect on the doctrine of salvation. If the soul goes to heaven at death, there is no real need for a pre-advent judgment, no real need for a second advent, no real need for overcoming the "sins of the flesh"—the soul can be saved without the body. It seems to me that this is one reason why much of Christianity puts such strong emphasis on justification and "have been saved," to the neglect or lack of emphasis on "being saved" and transformation through Christian growth. There is such a fear of "works" and "legalism" that predestination, predeterminism, or "once saved, always saved" quite easily follows. It is no wonder that so-called Christian communities and congregations have drifted into a secularism and worldliness that is a gross misrepresentation of the gospel. If one cannot be lost because of disobedience, why should one obey?

But what about the many uses of the words "everlasting life" and "eternal life" in the New Testament? Don't we have eternal life now? (We return to this question, which was briefly answered in Chapter 3.) Jesus said, "He who believes in the Son has eternal life . . ." (John 3:36). And John 5:24: "Truly, truly, I say to you, he who hears my word and believes him who sent me, has eternal life; he does not come into judgment,[9] but has passed from death to life." Having heard the words of Jesus, John later wrote, "And this is the testimony, that God gave us eternal life, and this life is in his Son. He who has the Son has life; he who has not the Son has not life. I write this to you who believe in the name of the Son of God, that you may know that you have eternal life" (1 John 5:11-13).

Several words in the New Testament have been translated either "everlasting" or "eternal":

1. A form of the word *aion,* which means "age" or "age lasting," as in the passages quoted above and in Matthew 19:16: "And behold, one came up to him, saying, 'Teacher, what good deed must I do, to have eternal *(aionion)* life?'" And John 3:16: "For God so loved the world that he gave his only Son, that whoever believes in him should not perish but have eternal *(aionion)* life" (translated "everlasting" in the KJV).

2. *Aidios,* which means "perpetual," is used twice as in Romans 1:20: ". . . God has shown it . . . namely, his eternal *(aidios)* power and deity. . . ." And Jude 6: ". . . have been kept by him in eternal *(aidios)* chains in the nether gloom until the judgment of the great day. . . ." (Here the word "eternal" *[aidios]* obviously does not mean "without end" because the chains keep them only until the judgment.)

The word for "life" used in the above statements is *zoe,* which, you will recall, is different from what we might call natural, physical, or animal life. *Zoe* signifies a *quality* of life that is spiritual and complete, and when used in the New Testament (i.e. "He who believes in the Son has eternal life *[zoen aionion])* it embodies all of the Christian ideals and virtues. It is the kind of life we have "in Christ" (i.e. "He who has the Son has life *[zoe]").* This is confirmed in John 5:24: "Truly, truly, I say to you, he who hears my word and believes him who sent me, has eternal life; he does not come into judgment, but has passed from death to life." Our condition without Christ is represented by "death," but when Christ becomes our Saviour the *quality of life* changes. We "pass from death to life." "And this is life eternal, that they know thee the only true God, and Jesus Christ whom thou hast sent" (John 17:3).

The only words which inherently mean "life not subject to death," "immortality," or "incorruptibility" are the words *athanasia* or *aphtharsia.* The word *thanatos* means "death." When the "a" prefix is added, as in *athanasia,* the meaning is "not subject to death." The same is true of the word "aphtharsia." This life without the possibility of death is to be bestowed at the Second Advent (see 1 Cor. 15:51-54, quoted above).

On the other hand, there are instances in the New Testament when the words *zoe* or *zoen aionion* mean "unending life" or "immortality." They do not carry that meaning inherently, but do so because of the context in which they are used. For instance, in Mark 10:31 eternal life is used in the sense of unending, immortal life because of the context—the age or world to come: ". . . who will not receive a hundredfold now in this time, houses and brothers and sisters and mothers and children and lands, with persecutions, and in the age to come eternal life." Or Titus 3:7 where the context is the hope of the saved: ". . . so that we might be justified by his grace and become heirs in hope of eternal life." An interesting relationship between *immortality* and *eternal life* is seen in Romans 2:6, 7 where the context is the judgment of God. "For he will render to every man according to his works: to those who by patience in well-doing seek for glory and honor and immortality, he will give eternal life. . . ."

Thus it is clear, we may have "eternal life" *now*—that quality of life that embodies all of the Christian ideals and virtues—as we seek for glory and honor and immortality. It is "by faith" in the promises of God that we "lay hold" *now* upon that eternal life which we hold as a title deed to that unending "immortal life" which God, *at the Second Coming,* will bestow upon those who love and serve Him. And what a comfort this is to all of us who have mourned the death and burial of loved ones we knew to be "in Christ"! Just as reconciliation is a gift from God at the beginning of the plan of salvation, immortality is a gift from God at the time of glorification.

Which answers the question, "What are we saved from?" In glorification we are saved from death.

The Gift of a Glorious Body

With the gift of immortality we would expect a change of body because who could or would want to live forever in the body we now possess? Well, a new body is exactly what is promised as a part of glorification. "But our commonwealth is in heaven, and from it we await a Savior, the Lord Jesus Christ, who will change our lowly body to be like his *glorious* body, by the power which enables him even to subject all things to himself" (Phil. 3:20, 21).

As we have seen, God did not create Adam and Eve immortal. They were subject to death. It would seem, however, that His ultimate purpose was to have an immortal mankind more fully "in His image" bodily. Note what we read in 1 Cor. 15:35-50: "But some one will ask, 'How are the dead raised? With what kind of body do they come?' You foolish man! What you sow does not come to life unless it dies. And what you sow is not the body which is to be, but a bare kernel, perhaps of wheat or of some other grain. But God gives it a body as he has chosen, and to each kind of seed its own body. For not all flesh is alike, but there is one kind for men, another for animals, another for birds, another for fish. There are celestial bodies and there are terrestrial bodies; but the glory of the celestial is one, and the glory of the terrestrial is another. There is the one glory of the sun, and another glory of the moon, another glory of the stars; for star differs from star in glory.

"So is it with the resurrection of the dead. What is sown is perishable, what is raised is imperishable. It is sown in dishonor, it is raised in glory. It is sown in weakness, it is raised in power. It is sown a physical body, it is raised a spiritual body. If there is a physical body, there is also a spiritual body. Thus it is written, 'The first man Adam became a living being'; the last Adam became a life-giving spirit. But it is not the spiritual which is first but the physical, and then the spiritual. The first man was from the earth, a man of dust; the second man is from heaven. As was the man of dust, so are those who are of dust; and as is the man of heaven, so are those who are of heaven. Just as we have borne the image of the man of dust, we shall also bear the image of the man of heaven. I tell you this, brethren: flesh and blood cannot inherit the kingdom of God, nor does the perishable inherit the imperishable."

I will have to leave it with the biologists to figure all that out, but two things seem clear: 1. "It is sown in dishonor, it is raised in *glory*." 2. "It is sown a physical body, it is raised a spiritual body." But in either case it is a body. We are not to become disembodied spirits, a thousand of which can dance on the head of a pin.

Be that as it may, isn't the future glorious? Salvation is more than reconciliation, justification, and transformation. Without glorification it's not worth the bother. I have a wonderful son who has been justified and is being transformed; he's growing day by day into Christlikeness. But he has multiple sclerosis. Thank God, the day is coming when he will be given a perfect, glorious spiritual body! And you don't know what that means unless you've been there.

Paul sees his life coming to an end. In his letter to Timothy he says something that deserves our attention and our appreciation: ". . . the time of my departure has come. I have fought the good fight, I have finished the race, I have kept the faith. Henceforth there is laid up for me the crown of righteousness, which the Lord, the righteous judge, will award to me on that Day, and not to me only but also to all who have loved his appearing" (2 Tim. 4:6-8). Did Paul try really hard? Is he rewarded for his effort? Is there merit in what he did? Is he assured of his salvation? Why? Because what he did, he did "in Christ." In his life and ministry, faith was energized by love through Jesus Christ, his Lord. Pressing toward the mark for the high calling of God in Christ Jesus is what he would encourage us all to do.

Restoration

9

Restoration

The Grey family has been in heaven but a short time. Grandfathers and grandmothers and one child were resurrected, and father, mother, and the other two children were translated. They have been taken to their home that Jesus has prepared for them, but now they have come to worship and are standing before the throne of God. The One seated on the throne appears like jasper and carnelian, and around the throne is a rainbow that looks like an emerald. Also around the throne are twenty-four thrones, and seated on the thrones are twenty-four elders, clad in white garments, with golden crowns upon their heads. From the throne issue flashes of lightning and voices and peals of thunder, and before the throne burn seven torches of fire, which are the seven spirits of God; and before the throne is a sea of glass, like crystal.

Around the throne, on each side, are four living creatures, full of eyes in front and behind: the first living creature is like a lion, the second like an ox, the third has the face of a man, and the fourth is like a flying eagle. And the four living creatures, each with six wings, are full of eyes all around and within, and day and night they never cease to sing,

"Holy, holy, holy, is the Lord God Almighty, who was and is and is to come!"

And whenever the living creatures give glory and honor and thanks to Him who is seated on the throne, who lives for ever and ever, the twenty-four elders fall down before Him who is seated on the throne and worship Him who lives for ever and ever; they cast their crowns before the throne, singing,

"Worthy art thou, our Lord and God,

to receive glory and honor and power,

for thou didst create all things,

and by thy will they exist and were created" (see Rev. 4:2-11).

And on Mount Zion stands the Lamb of God with the hundred and forty-four thousand who had His name and His Father's name written on their foreheads. And a voice from heaven is heard that sounds like many waters and loud thunder and like harpers playing on their harps, and they sing a new song before the throne and before the four living creatures and before the elders. No one could learn that song except the hundred and forty-four thousand who had been redeemed from the earth (see Rev. 14:1-3).

The Greys are part of the great multitude which no man could number, from every nation, from all tribes and peoples and tongues, which stand on the sea of glass before the throne and before the Lamb, clothed in white robes, with palm branches in their hands, and crying out with a loud voice, "Salvation belongs to our God who sits upon the throne, and to the Lamb!" And all the angels stand around the throne and around the elders and the four living creatures, and they fall on their faces before the throne and worship God, saying, "Amen! Blessing and glory and wisdom and thanksgiving and honor and power and might be to our God for ever and ever! Amen!" (see Rev. 7:9-12).

And the great multitude cries:

"Hallelujah! Salvation and glory and power belong to our God,

for his judgments are true and just;

He has judged the great harlot who corrupted the earth with her fornication,

and he has avenged on her the blood of his servants."

And once more they cry:

"Hallelujah! The smoke from her goes up for ever and ever."

And the twenty-four elders and the four living creatures fall down and worship God who is seated on the throne, saying, "Amen. Hallelujah!" And from the throne comes a voice crying,

"Praise our God, all you his servants,

you who fear him, small and great."

Then the voice of the great multitude, like the sound of many waters and like the sound of mighty thunderpeals, cries,

"Hallelujah! For the Lord our God the Almighty reigns.

Let us rejoice and exult and give him the glory,

for the marriage of the Lamb has come,

and his bride has made herself ready;

it was granted her to be clothed with fine linen, bright and pure" (see Rev. 19:1-8).

With harps of God in their hands, the Greys and those who had conquered the beast and its image and the number of its name, sing the song of Moses, the servant of God, and the song of the Lamb, saying,

"Great and wonderful are thy deeds,

O Lord God the Almighty!

Just and true are thy ways,

O King of the ages!

Who shall not fear and glorify thy name, O Lord?

For thou alone art holy.

All nations shall come and worship thee,

for thy judgments have been revealed" (see Rev. 15:2-4).

What a wonderful time of celebration and worship!

Since leaving earth, the Greys have been filled with unspeakable joy. Not only is their home a thorough delight, but they have met so many dear friends and relatives and rejoiced with them. They have also been thrilled beyond belief because they have seen and met many of the great heroes of the Bible—Noah, Abraham, David, Isaiah, Matthew, Mark, Luke, John, and Paul to name a few. And the great champions of faith—those missionaries and evangelists who have given their lives in service and obedience that others throughout the world might come to a knowledge of the Christ and be their neighbors in the New Jerusalem. And the spiritual leaders and reformers who refused to compromise and adulterate the Word of God, keeping the church moving toward the restoration of biblical truth.

The Greys, with the redeemed, will spend a thousand years in heaven in a work of judgment. "Blessed and holy is he who shares in the first resurrection! Over such the second death has no power, but they shall be priests of God and of Christ, and they shall reign with him a thousand years" (Rev. 20:6). They are to know why those whom they thought should be in heaven are not, and why those whom they thought wouldn't be are. There are no secrets when it comes to the judgment. The redeemed will have no reason to doubt God's love and grace throughout eternity.

But heaven is not "home." They belong on earth. God knows that, and it is His plan and purpose to restore what was lost in Eden. How He plans to do this is both glorious and tragic.

First the glorious: "Then I saw a new heaven and a new earth; for the first heaven and the first earth had passed away, and the sea was no more. And I saw the holy city, new Jerusalem, coming down out of heaven from God, prepared as a bride adorned for her husband; and I heard a loud voice from the throne saying, 'Behold, the dwelling of God is with men. He will dwell with them, and they shall be his people, and God himself will be with them; he will wipe away every tear from their eyes, and death shall be no more, neither shall there be mourning nor crying nor pain any more, for the former things have passed away.'

"And he who sat upon the throne said, 'Behold, I make all things new.' And he said, 'Write this, for these words are trustworthy and true.' And he said to me, '*It is done!* I am the Alpha and the Omega, the beginning and the end. To the thirsty I will give from the fountain of the water of life without payment. He who conquers shall have this heritage, and I will be his God and he shall be my son'" (Rev. 21:1-7). It all begins with "It is finished," at the cross, and it ends with "It is done!" when "the dwelling of God is with men."

Now the tragic: "'But as for the cowardly, the faithless, the polluted, as for murderers, fornicators, sorcerers, idolaters, and all liars, their lot shall be in the lake that burns with fire and sulphur, which is the second death'" (v. 8). And how this will transpire is portrayed for us in Rev. 20:7-10: "And when the thousand years are ended, Satan will be loosed from his prison and will come out to deceive the nations which are at the four corners of the earth, that is, Gog and Magog, to gather them for battle; their number is like the sand of the sea. And they marched up over the broad earth and surrounded the camp of the saints and the beloved city; but fire came down from heaven and consumed them, and the devil who had deceived them was thrown into the lake of fire and sulphur where the beast and the false prophet were, and they will be tormented day and night forever and ever." This is the hell of which Jesus spoke, the fire that never shall be quenched (Mark 9:43-48). This does not mean that the fire will never go out. But it will not be quenched until it devours whatever is to be burned. According to Malachi 4:1-3, "For behold, the day comes, burning like an oven, when all the arrogant and all evildoers will be stubble; the day that comes shall burn them up, says the Lord of hosts, so that it will leave them neither root not branch. But for you who fear my name the sun of righteousness shall rise, with healing in its wings. You shall go forth leaping like calves from the stall. And you shall tread down the wicked, for they will be ashes under the soles of your feet, on the day when I act, says the Lord of hosts." Again, the "forever and ever" mentioned above is from *eis tous aionas ton aionon,* which does not inherently mean time without end. (See previous discussion of this terminology in Chapter 8.)

What a sad day! God does not destroy the wicked with pleasure. According to Isaiah, His judgment is His strange act. "For the Lord shall rise up as in mount Perazim, he shall be wroth as in the valley of Gibeon, that he may do his work, his strange work; and bring to pass his act, his strange act" (28:21, KJV). We read in Lamentation 3:33: ". . . though he cause grief, he will have compassion according to the abundance of his steadfast love: for he does not willingly afflict or grieve the sons of men."

To restore the earth, the first earth must pass away. The Bible does not portray a hell somewhere beneath the earth that burns without end, where the wicked will cry for mercy which will never be granted. What would be the purpose? Is it there so that the redeemed can look in now and then and be frightened into continued obedience without sin? Or is it there for God to look into and find satisfaction in His justice? No, He says, "Behold, I make all things new."

As the life given to mankind in the beginning was the "good life," just so the "good life" will be restored, as prophesied before the first advent of Christ by Isaiah in Chapter 65:

"For behold, I create new heavens and a new earth; and the former things shall not be remembered or come into mind. But be glad and rejoice for ever in that which I create; for behold, I create Jerusalem a rejoicing, and her people a joy. I will rejoice in Jerusalem, and be glad in my people; no more shall be heard in it the sound of weeping and the cry of distress. No more shall there be in it an infant that lives but a few days, or an old man who does not fill out his days, for the child shall die a hundred years old, and the sinner a hundred years old shall be accursed. They shall build houses and inhabit them; they shall plant vineyards and eat their fruit. They shall not build and another inhabit; they shall not plant and another eat; for like the days of a tree shall the days of my people be, and my chosen shall long enjoy the work of their hands. They shall not labor in vain, or bear children in calamity; for they shall be the offspring of the blessed of the Lord, and their children with them. Before they call I will answer, while they are yet speaking I will hear. The wolf and the lamb shall feed together, the lion shall eat straw like the ox; and dust shall be the serpent's food. They shall not hurt or destroy in all my holy mountain, says the Lord" (vv. 17-25).

Seems too good to be true, doesn't it? But it's not. Continuing in Revelation 21, 22, John paints a similar portrait. I quote at length because it's such wonderful good news I hardly know where to quit. I need the blessed hope. Perhaps you do too.

"And in the Spirit he carried me away to a great, high mountain, and showed me the holy city Jerusalem coming down out of heaven from God, having the glory of God, its radiance like a most rare jewel, like a jasper, clear as crystal. It has a great, high wall, with twelve gates, and at the gates twelve angels, and on the gates the names of the twelve tribes of the sons of Israel were inscribed; on the east three gates, and on the north three gates, on the south three gates, and on the west three gates. And the wall of the city had twelve foundations, and on them the twelve names of the twelve apostles of the Lamb.

"And he who talked to me had a measuring rod of gold to measure the city and its gates and walls. The city lies four-square, its length the same as its breadth; and he measured the city with his rod, twelve thousand stadia; its length and breadth and height are equal. He also measured its wall, a hundred and forty-four cubits by a man's measure, that is, an angel's. The wall was built of jasper, while the city was pure gold, clear as glass. The foundations of the wall of the city were adorned with every jewel; the first was jasper, the second sapphire, the third agate, the fourth emerald, the fifth onyx, the sixth carnelian, the seventh chrysolite, the eighth beryl, the ninth topaz, the tenth chrysoprase, the eleventh jacinth, the twelfth amethyst. And the twelve gates were twelve pearls, each of the gates made of a single pearl, and the street of the city was pure gold, transparent as glass.

"And I saw no temple in the city, for its temple is the Lord God the Almighty and the Lamb. And the city has no need of sun or moon to shine upon it, for the glory of God is its light, and its lamp is the Lamb. By its light shall the nations walk; and the kings of the earth ring their glory into it, and its gates shall never be shut by day—and there shall be no night there; they shall bring into it the glory and the honor of the nations. But nothing unclean shall enter it, nor any one who practices abomination or falsehood, but only those who are written in the Lamb's book of life" (Rev. 21:10-27).

"Then he showed me the river of the water of life, bright as crystal, flowing from the throne of God and the Lamb through the middle of the street of the city; also, on either side of the river, the tree of life with its twelve kinds of fruit, yielding its fruit each month; and the leaves of the tree were for the healing of the nations. There shall no more be anything accursed, but the throne of God and of the Lamb shall be in it, and his servants shall worship him; they shall see his face, and his name shall be on their foreheads. And night shall be no more; they need no light of lamp or sun, for the Lord God will be their light, and they shall reign for ever and ever" (22:1-5).

From these two portraits we learn the following:

1. A new heaven and a new earth is to be created with Jerusalem as its center.

2. The New Jerusalem is a bride prepared for her husband, which brings to mind an interesting analogy found in Ephesians 5:25-27: "Husbands, *love your wives, as Christ loved the church* and gave himself up for her, that he might sanctify her, having cleansed her by the washing of water with the word, that he might present the church to himself in splendor, without spot or wrinkle or any such thing, that she might be holy and without blemish." Here the "church" is portrayed as a wife or bride being prepared for presentation to Christ.

Applying that analogy, we may say the New Jerusalem is a corporate representation of God's people; His "church," a "bride" without spot or wrinkle, holy and without blemish, presented to God in splendor, thus fulfilling Christ's desire.

3. As the bride, the church has a blessed relationship with God. Isaiah portrays it as one of rejoicing, joy, and gladness: "Before they call I will answer, while they are yet speaking I will hear" (65:24). John's portrayal adds to the glory of this relationship between God and His bride, the New Jerusalem: "Behold, the dwelling of God is with men. He will dwell with them, and they shall be his people, and God himself will be with them" (Rev. 21:3). The temple is the Lord God the Almighty and the Lamb. The nations of the earth shall walk in the light of the city and bring their glory and honor into it. The unclean and the wicked shall not enter it, only those who are written in the Lamb's book of life. The servants of God

and of the Lamb shall worship Him, and they shall see His face. His name shall be in their foreheads and they shall reign forever and ever. *In the New Jerusalem and the new earth there will be no God-independence*—"Who is God that I should be mindful of Him?"

4. The husband clothes the New Jerusalem, his bride, in extravagant splendor: The "city" is radiant like a most rare jewel, like a jasper, clear as crystal. The wall is built of jasper, while the city is pure as gold. The foundations of the city are adorned with twelve precious jewels. Each of the twelve gates is made of a single pearl, and the street is pure gold, "transparent as glass."

5. The life expectancy of the redeemed is not clearly stated in Isaiah. The terminology does not indicate immortality. It might be said that Isaiah did not use this terminology because Christ had not yet come. According to Paul, it was ". . . our Savior Christ Jesus, who abolished death and *brought life and immortality to light through the gospel"* (2 Tim. 1:10b). Thus, in Revelation, it can be said with certainty that "death shall be no more," and "they shall reign for ever and ever."

6. Isaiah describes the "good life" in classic and memorable terms: "They shall build houses and inhabit them; they shall plant vineyards and eat their fruit. . . . They shall not labor in vain, or bear children in calamity." How many of us have worked for the comfort and well-being of others while we could not afford such for ourselves? I was born with a liking for milk and have never overcome it. But during the Great Depression we lived in the city, and our milk was delivered by the milkman—one quart a day. I never got to drink as much as I wanted. Then one day we went to my uncle's dairy farm. He had cows, a number of them. They gave milk, lots of it. As I watched them being milked, and as buckets of

milk poured into a large can, I thought, "Wow, now I'll drink until I can drink no more!" So at dinner that evening I decided to quickly drain the glass of milk set before me so that I could have another. But there was not to be another. "What? Just one glass? What do you do with all that milk your cows give? I saw buckets of it being poured into large cans!" My question was answered by the explanation that most of the milk had to be sold to provide for the other necessities of life. What a rotten deal! All those beautiful cows, and someone else gets to drink all the milk! I have thought since how wonderful it will be to live in a new earth, in a land that "flows with milk and honey," where we will not have to do all the milking while others drink all the milk!

I remember preaching a sermon one time in which I used this illustration, and after the worship service as I shook hands with the people who were leaving, one brother took my hand and said, "You forget. Milk is not a health food. There will be no milk in heaven." To which I replied, "O yes there will be! In heaven, milk will be a health food!" We both laughed and enjoyed the humor.

Animal lovers, take heed! Not only will the wolf and the lamb feed together and the lion eat straw like the ox, but according to Isaiah 11:6, ". . . the leopard shall lie down with the kid, and the calf and the lion and the fatling together, and a little child shall lead them."

And according to the Revelation, there will be no more tears, no pain, no crying. The city has no need of sun or moon, for the glory of God is its light, and its lamp is the Lamb. Its gates will never be shut by day, and there will be no night there. The river of water of life flows from the throne of God and the Lamb, and the tree of life grows on either side of the river. *This is not only Eden restored; it is Eden restored, and so much more!*

The New Jerusalem is not new because of when it is created. It is new because it represents this new relationship between God and His people. "Tell me, you who desire to be under law, do you not hear the law? For it is written that Abraham had two sons, one by a slave and one by a free woman. But the son of the slave was born according to the flesh, the son of the free woman through promise. Now this is an allegory: these women are two covenants. One is from Mount Sinai, bearing children for slavery; she is Hagar. Now Hagar is Mount Sinai in Arabia; she corresponds to the present Jerusalem, for she is in slavery with her children. But the *Jerusalem above* is free, and she is our mother. . . . Now we, brethren, like Isaac, are *children of promise"* (Gal. 4:21-26, 28).

Quite obviously, the New Jerusalem of Revelation 21 is the Jerusalem above. She is the bride, the mother of *the children of promise.* The *New Jerusalem* is at the center of *righteousness by faith.*

"Behold, the dwelling of God is with men. He will dwell with them, and they shall be his people, and God himself will be with them." Of all that has been said in the chapters of this book about a salvation full and complete, this is the bottom line. From alienation to reconciliation, from rebellion to transformation, from mortality to immortality, from unspeakably tragic loss to a restoration that is more than complete, we shall be His people—by grace, through faith. "Salvation belongs to God and to the Lamb." Blessing and glory and wisdom and thanksgiving and honor and power and might belong to Him. Amen!

"Therefore, since we are justified by faith, we have peace with God through our Lord Jesus Christ. Through him we have obtained access to this grace in which we stand, and we rejoice in our hope of sharing the glory of God" (Rom. 5:1, 2).

I plan to share that glory. Come, share the glory with me.

Endnotes

[1] Luke 23:34; Mark 15:34; Luke 23:46; John 19:30.

[2] See *The Analytical Greek Lexicon* by Wesley J. Perschbacher.

[3] The Greek *sozomenois,* translated "who are being saved," is a present passive participle indicating continuous action.

[4] In the Greek the critical word sequence is *hina en auto auxethete eis soterian,* which means "in order that in it you may grow into (or to or up to) salvation."

[5] There were those who were critical of Paul's ministry, teaching, and authority because of his background. But Paul considered some "of repute" more than others (apparently the apostles who had been disciples of Christ, which are mentioned in verse 9).

[6] Peter does not retaliate and oppose Paul, but in the spirit of Christian brotherhood acknowledges his wisdom in 2 Peter 3:15, 16, while observing that he writes some things "hard to understand."

[7] See James 1:19, 21, 26; 1 Peter 2:13, 18; 3:9, 10-12; 1 John 3:11, 12, 17, 18.

[8] For my original article with references on this subject, see "The Doctrine of Sin in I John" in *Andrews University Seminary Studies,* vol. 25, no. 1, Spring 1987, Berrien Springs, MI: Andrews University Press.

For an extensive survey of the literature see Leon Eloy Wade, "Impeccability in I John: An Evaluation," (Ph.D. dissertation, Andrews University, 1986).

[9] He has been justified and does not come into the judgment of the unsaved, but, having been born again, has passed from death to life.